Client/Server Application Development

Tools and Techniques

Computer Technology Research Corp.
6 North Atlantic Wharf, Charleston, South Carolina 29401 U.S.A.
Telephone: (803) 853-6460 • Fax: (803) 853-7210
E-mail: CTReditors@aol.com or CompuServe 75213,3152

Client/Server Application Development: Tools and Techniques

Copyright © Computer Technology Research Corp.

First Edition – 1995
Update Edition – 1996
ISBN 1-56607-033-3 ✓

Published by Computer Technology Research Corp., Charleston, South Carolina U.S.A.

Library of Congress Cataloging-in-Publication Data

Client/server application development: tools and techniques -- 1st ed.
    p. cm.
  ISBN 1-56607-033-3
  1. Client/server computing 2. Application software I. Title.
QA76.9.C55L45 1994
005.2--dc20

94-21113
CIP

Client/Server
Application Development
Tools and Techniques

TABLE OF CONTENTS

APPENDICES

LIST OF TABLES

LIST OF FIGURES

Introduction

As client/server (C/S) computing catches on in the business world, application development (AD) is becoming a problem. More and more mission-critical data is being delivered to end-users through local area networks (LANs), and this data is increasingly residing on LAN servers. Management information systems (MIS) workers must spend more time developing applications for this mission-critical data.

However, AD in the C/S environment is not a straightforward task. The definition of C/S itself is not clear; there are several types of C/S deployment, and application tools for each activity in C/S abound.

This report presents a definition of C/S and examines various issues surrounding AD and the actual AD tools. It includes several examples and illustrations and is based on a combination of extensive independent research and personal interviews with information technology (IT) professionals.

This report is divided into 13 chapters and two appendices:

1 –   Executive Summary
2 –   A Look at the Client/Server Environment
3 –   Application Development, Part I
4 –   Application Development, Part II

Chapter 1 gives an overview of C/S terminology, the requirements for developing applications in the C/S environment, and the various types of development tools available.

Chapter 2 provides a detailed examination of first and second generation C/S environments and discusses factors to be considered when implementing a C/S system.

Chapter 3 defines and discusses C/S AD environments and projects the future of these environments. It considers the features C/S AD environments should have, and discusses some of their respective advantages and disadvantages.

Chapter 4 discusses some considerations when developing applications for C/S environments, and the advantages and disadvantages of using workgroup development teams. It provides suggestions on selecting the ideal development team and discusses some methodologies for AD. Finally, this chapter explores the question of standardization and the corporate application programming interface (API).

Chapter 5 examines some of the things that can go wrong when developing applications in a C/S environment.

Chapter 6 discusses middleware and how it functions, including message-oriented middleware and remote procedure calls (RPCs).

Chapter 7 discusses the requirements for testing and illustrates some of the difficulties of testing in a C/S environment. Also discussed in this chapter are different types of testing, including a list of questions testers should ask themselves. Learn how to design test cases, what to look for in testing tools, and the questions of how to implement automated testing. This chapter also discusses the advantages and disadvantages of automation and lists some of the testing tools on the market.

Chapter 8 discusses computer-aided software engineering (CASE) tools. It looks at upper-CASE, lower-CASE, integrated-CASE, and CASE for maintenance. This chapter also explores the concept of the repository, and compares active and passive repositories. The chapter discusses the concept of standards for repositories, examines the merging of CASE and AD tools, and provides a list of CASE tools.

Chapter 9 focuses fourth-generation languages (4GLs). It discusses 4GLs and lists some of the 4GL available AD tools.

Chapter 10 probes object-oriented programming (OOP) and its advantages and disadvantages. The questions of retraining business organizations for OOP and a standard for object technology (OT) are also discussed. The use of OT to leverage legacy systems is also mentioned, as are tips for surviving OOP projects. Finally, this chapter discusses key functions for OOP AD tools and lists object tools.

Chapter 11 discusses several types of AD tools, including graphical, network, and miscellaneous AD tools. It offers suggestions for developing superior graphical user interfaces (GUIs) and cross-platform tools, and lists some graphical development/GUI development tools and cross-platform development tools.

As applications are developed, distribution can be a problem. In some organizations, they are physically distributed on disks which must be loaded into the system. This leads to the next problem: version control. Developers must ensure the same version of an application is on their users' computers or they will spend time on maintenance. Purchasing an electronic software distribution (ESD) package will resolve many of the problems.

Chapter 12 explores the concept of ESD and its market segments. It cautions against the pitfalls of buying an ESD package, demonstrates how to plan for ESD purchases, and lists some ESD vendors.

Chapter 13, the Conclusion, ties together the ideas presented in this report. MIS should bear in mind that it is better to plan in advance, before beginning development work, than to just jump in and begin. This chapter discusses the appropriate long-term plan, selecting the right development environment, and building the right development team. Testing early and often, standardizing as extensively as possible, and deciding which methodology to use (depending on whether corporate legacy resources are to be leveraged) will help when developing applications.

There are also two appendices. Appendix A is a glossary of C/S terminology, geared toward AD. Appendix B is a list of the references for this report, many of which will provide detailed information on specific aspects discussed herein.

Chapter 1

Executive Summary

To develop applications in the client/server (C/S) environment, MIS should understand what C/S is: it is a subset of cooperative processing, in which the server and client processors synchronize on a task through the use of remote procedure calls (RPCs).

According to Stamford, Connecticut-based market research firm, The Gartner Group, Inc., there are five basic styles of C/S processing. All the styles address the same issue: the application, presentation, and data access logic must be logically separated. They can reside on the same physical box; however size or power is, within reason, not necessarily the means used to define which box should be the client and which the server. It is possible to have a UNIX box as the server and a mainframe as the client, for example.

It is important to step back and take a look at the bigger picture. Too often, C/S pilot systems fail when scaled up and implemented within the corporation. Because they lack scalability, they are not flexible enough to meet the needs of the corporation as a whole or fail to meet the demands of the software lifecycle and make programmers work more than they should.

Corporations must realize tools are paramount to developing client/server applications. When developing applications, there are three critical implementation issues: what is required to develop applications, what types of tools are available, and the development of a strategic plan based on the corporate strategic plan.

Very often, C/S applications are developed by business workgroups on the grounds they understand business processes better than the MIS staff. They understand business processes well, but lack the MIS discipline which leads to reusable, maintainable applications which will fit into the MIS strategy and help further the corporate business strategy.

This, then, implies strategy for AD is important. Instead of merely acquiring the tools, MIS should consider toolsets, and should then examine these toolsets to ensure they constitute a complete AD environment.

An AD environment should have scalability, flexibility, and programmer-productivity technologies and offer lifecycle support. This will enable developers to build applications which will have a life beyond the pilot. Also, corporations should select their development teams carefully, including MIS staff among them to give the group direction and guide it in MIS disciplines.

There are various methodologies used in AD. This report looks at rapid AD and the older waterfall methodology, as well as the three-tier development approach.

Once the development environment (and hence the tools) has been identified, the development team has been set-up, and the methodology selected, MIS should look at implementing AD standards through the creation of a corporate API and enforcing it. This will ensure all applications developed will adhere to a set of standards so users will learn them more quickly and require less training, thus making maintenance easier.

When the corporate application programming interface (API) is established and enforced, the respective duties of central MIS and line MIS will need to be clarified. An arbitration panel consisting of senior representatives from all departments should be set-up to arbitrate any disputes.

The development team can then examine the development work. It should consider the function and purpose of middleware, which includes RPCs, and the communications between the back-end and the front-end. The team may then want to consider whether to use RPCs or message-oriented middleware, which will possibly open up new avenues.

The development team should then consider the need for testing and plan for that testing. Testing should begin as early as possible in the development process; some say testing plans should be drawn up at the same time as AD plans so the quality of the applications can be assured.

The question of whether to automate testing should also be examined. Automation speeds-up testing and enables more thorough testing than manual processes; it also allows programmers to be more productive.

Many large vendors offer AD tools with their system software, but this does not mean these tools are the best available. Often, smaller, independent software vendors (ISVs) produce more leading-edge software, simply because that is the tool to help them get into the market.

Nine leading ISVs, all specializing in leading-edge software development tools and solutions, have formed the ISV Coalition for Software Productivity through Open Systems. This organization was formed to promote open systems solutions from ISVs and to help software developers, engineers, and managers obtain complete information on all available development tool options before making a purchase decision. The ISV Coalition members are listed in Table 1.1.

Table 1.1 Independent Software Vendor Coalition for Software Productivity through Open Systems

Alsys, Inc.* (San Diego, California)
Atria Software (Natick, Massachusetts)
CaseWare, Inc. (Irvine, California)
CenterLine Software, Inc. (Cambridge, Massachusetts)
Expersoft (San Diego, California)
Imperial Software Technology (Berkshire, United Kingdom)
Integrated Computer Solutions (ICS), Inc. (Cambridge, Massachusetts)
IXI Ltd. (Cambridge, United Kingdom)
Lucid, Inc. (Menlo Park, California)

* formerly Telesoft

The tools themselves must then be considered. There are CASE tools, which have been quite popular for a long time. CASE methodology depends on the data dictionary or the repository (a dictionary with added features) that manipulates and analyzes data. With the growing corporate trend to make data a profit center rather than a cost center, the concept of a corporate data repository is gaining ground.

There is one problem with selecting CASE tools: repositories from different vendors do not communicate with each other. This has prevented the development of corporation-wide repositories.

Each vendor is developing its own API and the number of APIs in the market is proliferating and fragmenting the market. There are two industry initiatives which may provide a long-term solution to this problem. One is the development of an industry-wide standard data interchange format among CASE tools, and the other is the framework for an open system repository.

Whether these initiatives will work, however, depends on Microsoft Corporation, which rules the desktop. Already, Microsoft and Texas Instruments, Inc. (TI) have announced they will jointly develop an open, scalable, C/S repository which will be object-based so pieces of it can be changed quickly. This announcement is seen by many as a bid by these two firms to gain a stranglehold on the market.

There is also the 4GL technology. These tools have evolved to the point where they incorporate GUIs and C/S technology, offer rapid prototyping, and are being linked with other tools for C/S AD.

The question of object-oriented technology remains. This has often been hailed as the new paradigm, and many organizations have been talking about how quickly and easily they have developed applications with OT. OT does have its drawbacks, however, not the least of which is the high cost of retraining mainframe programmers. The watchword here, then, is caution.

Whether corporate AD teams are designing CASE, 4GL or object-oriented applications, the push now is to offer graphical front-ends. GUIs are popular – they are the basis on which Microsoft Windows soared. They are easy to learn and require less user training than character-based interfaces.

Developing GUI applications, however, is no easy task. There are far more variables than in character-based interfaces and testing is much more difficult. Also, developing GUI applications requires a large degree of discipline because some programmers try to use all the available elements. This results in a lack of standardization among the icons, colors, and other elements of the screen.

Version control becomes very important as programmers begin developing an application, rolling it out to testing teams, and pushing out the pilot. Programmers must know which version of the application each user has on his or her desktop. The question of software distribution is also a problem. Often, people take what is known as the "Sneakernet" approach – walking over to each terminal and physically installing the software.

A better solution is to turn to ESD. Most ESD packages have a "discovery feature," which goes to each desktop on a network, discovers what software is running and the hardware configuration, and stores this information. Upgrading the version of an application becomes simple, as does distributing the software. Again, turning to automation in these tasks frees up programmers to do what is really important – program.

Chapter 2

A Look at the Client/Server Environment

Overview

C/S is a subset of cooperative processing. It involves two processors – the client and the server – working cooperatively on a single task. The processors are synchronized by RPCs.

This is how C/S differs from host-based processing, where the host does most of the actual processing. In a C/S system, the presentation logic, the application logic, and the data access logic are separated. This need not be a physical separation; it can be a logical separation, which means all three logic elements can run on the same processor in different logical partitions. There are various ways of partitioning the three components of C/S, but the presentation logic must always execute or run on the client system.

Further, C/S does not necessarily include GUIs or open systems. From the technical point of view, it is possible to implement a C/S system with a character-based interface, although this is far less user-friendly than the GUI. It is possible to have a C/S system based on a proprietary operating environment, although increasingly, users are looking toward open systems, to be independent of any one particular software or hardware vendor.

There are, then, two definitions of C/S, both of which must be considered: the objective, technical definition based on technical requirements and the

---

subjective definition based on a corporation's needs and will include GUIs and requirements for open systems. While the objective definition is standard, the subjective definition will vary from corporation to corporation, although most organizations will include requirements for GUIs and open systems specifications.

Definition of Client/Server

C/S processing is a subset of cooperative processing. Typically, it involves two processors working cooperatively, synchronized by RPCs. Although several clients are connected to one server, only one client works with the server at any point in time.

As stated, a C/S system has three components: presentation logic (often a GUI), application logic, and data access logic. Physically separating the three components of a C/S system is called "application partitioning." When applications are partitioned, the presentation logic must always execute on the client. Whether the application logic executes on the client or the server depends on available resources and which solution is most efficient.

There is no easy way to distinguish between the client and the server portions of an application. Command interpretation, help processing, and as much data input validation as possible should be performed by the client because they are all highly interactive activities. Application logic, error handling, transaction preparation, and transaction validation can be handled either by the client or the server, depending on what the user wants out of an application.

The Gartner Group, Inc. has defined, in a very simplistic form, five styles of C/S computing according to how application components are split between client and server systems. These are:

1) Distributed presentation;
2) Remote presentation;
3) Distributed logic;
4) Remote data management; and
5) Distributed data management.

These five styles are shown in Figure 2.1. The figure shows only one server; in reality, there could be servers of servers in a multitiered architecture or there could be a forked architecture, where a client invokes multiple servers directly.

The aforementioned constitutes the objective, technical definition of the term *client/server*. Here, the term means a specific concept in data processing and can be applied equally by anyone in any organization.

To recapitulate, C/S refers to the separation of the functional components of the traditional application, such as data access, application logic, and the presentation or interface. It is, therefore, a subset of distributed processing, and one in which the client and server are synchronized by means of RPCs.

There is, however, another definition of C/S, and this is where the trouble begins. This definition is a subjective one, where its meaning depends on what the user considers important. It varies from organization to organization.

Such a subjective definition is required because C/S means different things to different people, and their definition of C/S will include what is meaningful to them. For example, GUIs are often seen as an integral part of a C/S environment, and many corporations will not consider an environment as being truly C/S unless it includes GUIs. Technically, however, there is nothing stopping a corporation from using character-based interfaces. GUIs are, therefore, part of the subjective definition of C/S rather than the technical definition.

The Gartner Group, Inc. lists 10 guidelines for C/S computing in the C/S Profiles series of its Software Management Strategies report (see Table 2.1).

Figure 2.1 Five Methods of Client/Server Computing

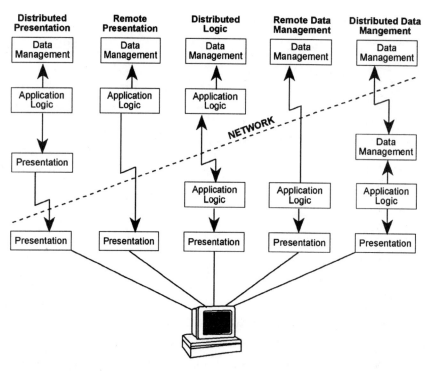

Source: Gartner Group

Considerations When Implementing Client/Server

When considering the implementation of a C/S system or moving to one off the mainframe, the main thing to remember will be the corporation's business needs. Before deciding on the hardware or software, the MIS department should base its strategy according to the corporate business plan.

Table 2.1 Guidelines for Client/Server Computing

1)	C/S computing is a cooperative processing architecture that involves the use of an intelligent workstation beyond terminal emulation.
2)	C/S is a separate idea from open systems and downsizing.
3)	C/S comprises five models: remote presentation, distributed presentation, distributed function, remote data management, and distributed data management.
4)	No single one of these models is intrinsically superior to any other; users should select the model that best suits their purposes.
5)	*Remoteness* does not equal *distance*: LAN and WAN issues have a great deal of influence on C/S deployment.
6)	C/S processing can complement other models (batch, monolithic online) through the sharing of data.
7)	Different C/S models can coexist in one application.
8)	The usual business driver of C/S is productivity, not cost reduction.
9)	The role of an intelligent workstation in C/S allows opportunities for integration of external data, local "groupware," and personal productivity technology such as spreadsheets.
10)	C/S represents a gradual inversion of the computing architecture with more control and decisions reverting to the user.

The MIS plan must ensure systems purchased and implemented will further the goals set out in the business plan. Productivity, not cost reduction, is the key. C/S systems are often more expensive than they initially appear. The question to be asked is, "How can we improve productivity by implementing C/S?," not "How can we cut costs through implementing C/S?" If a corporation's productivity can be improved by using personal computers (PCs) running Microsoft Windows, for example, these items should be purchased, rather than more expensive computers based on reduced instruction set computing (RISC) processors.

Notwithstanding the emphasis on productivity, moving to C/S can result in major savings, especially when a corporation is faced with the need to upgrade its legacy (mainframe-based) systems. The key here is to determine exactly what benefits are sought, to ensure they will be realized by moving to C/S, and to ensure existing infrastructure such as tape silos, for example, can be used in the new system as much as possible.

When it comes to quantifying the benefits of C/S, MIS must know what benefits to seek. Reference to the corporate strategy will help identify in which direction the organization is moving, and make it easier to work toward the kind of benefits which will fit in with these goals. For example, if a corporation wants to speed-up production in reaction to demand, one possible solution would be to give key decision makers executive information systems on the desktop. The benefit here would be to give the executives more access to vital information more quickly so they can react to changes in market demand more rapidly.

Chapter 3

Application Development, Part I

First- and Second-Generation Client/Server

First-generation C/S systems, most of which are pilot projects, are not robust enough to support real business applications in realtime. Market research firm The Meta Group of Westport, Connecticut, states first-generation C/S applications have simple application logic, single GUI support, no integration with other desktop applications, one C/S deployment architecture, a single concurrent data source, and low maintenance.

C/S is now in its *second* generation. The new C/S tools must support an environment which is heterogeneous and dynamic, and have the following characteristics: complex application logic, portability across multiple GUIs, complete integration with other desktop applications, cross-functional business processes, scalability from workgroup to enterprise systems, flexible C/S deployment options, portability across operating systems and hardware platforms, concurrent access to multiple data sources across heterogeneous platforms including relational and non-relational data, and application maintenance, configuration management, and version control.

First-generation C/S tools cannot meet the needs of decentralized organizations and distributed information systems because they are not robust enough to handle mission-critical business applications.

There is no single tool which satisfies all application requirements. However, some tools do meet a variety of requirements, and some other tools are not appropriate for delivering certain systems. To select the appropriate tools, developers must understand what kinds of applications need to be developed, how they will be executed and deployed, which business functions will be involved, and how production and corporate data will be staged and updated.

Choosing the Right Client/Server Application Development Environment

More important, perhaps, than selecting the right tool, is the question of selecting the appropriate C/S AD environment. Increasingly, MIS is seeing AD environments as essential to success in building distributed, open production system (according to a report by the Aberdeen Group, a market research firm based in Boston, Massachusetts).

What is a Client/Server Development Environment?

The Aberdeen Group lists the following criteria for considering a software development toolset to be a C/S AD environment:

- It must help in developing C/S applications. It must be a useful tool for developing application software on desktop clients/server, software on servers, or both.

- It must be open. The Aberdeen Group defines "openness" as interoperability, both with software from other vendors, and across platforms. An open C/S AD environment is multisupplier and multiplatform, and produces multisupplier and multiplatform applications.

- It must run on most of the common C/S networks. These include desktops and workstations on the client side, workstation, minicomputer and mainframe server hardware running a network operating system (OS), UNIX or a proprietary OS on the server side.

The Aberdeen Group also has conducted in-depth interviews of enterprises that have completed one or more commercial C/S applications. These interviews show most have several factors in common:

- They all started with a pilot project.

- The attitudes of most of the staffers in charge changed from reluctance or skepticism to dedication. Those who best understood the complexity of mainframe AD often became the greatest champions of C/S computing.

- Enterprise visibility was high. Initially, this led to fear of failure, but later it was seen as a positive factor when the projects succeeded or surpassed expectations.

- Cost justification was easy regardless of project size. High mainframe development operations chargebacks and costs made the task of cost-justifying C/S projects simple.

- Typically, expectations were exceeded in the major categories of cost reduction, time to complete, and economic payoff.

- Expectations were met in the categories of user productivity improvement and the ability of MIS to move up the learning curve.

- Expectations were typically not met in the categories of availability and maturity of tools, and the number and size of qualified suppliers.

- Alternatives to C/S AD tools took too long to develop, could not be done at any cost or were simply too expensive. For example, IBM's DB2 was usually considered, but rejected as too costly.

An effective C/S AD environment can deliver strategic benefits – it can increase end-user and programmer productivity, reduce end-user retraining costs, take advantage of low-cost desktop million instructions per second (MIPS), and decrease data center loads. Also, it can help in the migration of legacy applications, increase end-user satisfaction and interoperability, and increase MIS flexibility.

However, in many cases, the environments are not fully-featured, immature, and not attuned to the needs of large-scale information systems (IS) organizations. The choice of the right AD environment is strategically vital to effective long-term delivery of C/S benefits.

New Tasks for Client/Server Application Development Environments

Previously, many large-scale application developers focused on online transaction processing (OLTP). A typical C/S OLTP application might involve form fill-in, emphasize database updates, and have a GUI front-end replacing menu-driven or command-driven user interfaces. They typically tapped one database from one supplier.

Now, with the empowerment of the end-user, more and more new applications aim to support end-users carrying out large-scale decision making. This involves large doses of queries with a sprinkling of OLTP-style updates.

The new C/S applications typically act as funnels, gathering a broad range of data which is possibly relevant, filtering that data into useful information, delivering the information to the end-user, and presenting the data in a concise, meaningful way.

Today's AD environments must get data from multiple databases from multiple suppliers, then deliver it to clients through middleware, filter it on the server through stored procedures or on the client through data analysis tools, and present it to end-users using GUIs such as Microsoft Windows.

Meanwhile, the demand for fast development has increased. There are two reasons for this: the applications backlog is growing, and more mission-critical information is being put on C/S LANs.

Leaders of the Pack

The most popular C/S AD environments today, according to the Aberdeen Group, are:

- Structured Query Language (SQL) Windows 5.0 from Gupta Corp.

- Visual Basic 3.0 from Microsoft Corp.

- PowerBuilder 3.0 from Powersoft Corp.

PowerBuilder's revenues are growing at well over 100% per year; Gupta's revenues, including sales of the firm's SQLBase relational database management system (RDBMS) are up over 50% year to year; and Microsoft's Visual Basic has achieved "exceptionally high visibility" among suppliers, ISVs and IS shops. However, popularity is not enough.

What Client/Server Application Development Environments Should Have

Some of these environments raise serious long-term questions. Buyers should check them against four criteria: scalability, flexibility, software lifecycle support, and the availability of programmer productivity technology. The multitude of new tasks these environments must undertake means new C/S AD environments must have these four criteria.

Even the best C/S AD environments are not yet mature, and the Aberdeen Group recommends they be supplemented with other development tools such as upper-CASE design products, software distribution utilities or transaction processing monitor server-side toolsets. (For an explanation of upper-CASE, see Chapter 9.) The open flexibility of the new AD environments allows them to easily incorporate many of these third-party tools.

Scalability

The Aberdeen Group foresees a three- to five-fold increase in enterprise-scale query processing, OLTP, and batch demand over the next few years. The major driving force behind this will be the new model of decision making, with greater emphasis on empowerment of the end-user.

Meanwhile, new open parallel servers are allowing IS to scale raw performance cost-effectively, by adding more processors as required. RDBMSs redesigned to leverage the capabilities of parallel processors are achieving performance speed-up and data storage scale-up in terms of orders of magnitude. In other words, the hardware and software have improved to match future needs.

The bottleneck, then, is the ability to develop tools which are scalable, to match the hardware and software improvements – or lack of them. The scalability C/S AD environments should deliver has several dimensions:

• Performance scalability of the applications;

- Development-process scalability as the complexity of the application and the number of programmers required increases; and

- Leveraged scalability or the ability to leverage the new hardware and RDBMS technologies.

Performance Scalability

These are the factors affecting performance scalability:

- Native connections to a scalable RDBMS;

- The ability to interleave high-performance code in low-performance applications;

- Whether the C/S AD environment runtime code is interpreted or compiled, and if compiled, the maturity of the compiler technology;

- Database design, in data management applications;

- Object access methods, in object-oriented programs; and

- The scheduling of the application relative to other applications running simultaneously.

One factor unique to C/S AD environments has proven critical to application performance, and to the power and flexibility of the mechanism defining the amount of information communicated between client and server. Too much communication can consume bandwidth and kill application performance, and the Aberdeen Group recommends the AD environment give the programmer maximum control over C/S communications.

Development-Process Scalability

IS shops in large enterprises may create large-scale mission-critical applications, but the AD environments available today do not yet fully incorporate data center-type technologies for handling AD on such a scale. Such data center-type technologies include:

- *Repositories.* These are common storage areas for programs, program information, and statistics. Repositories can be a valuable source of information for project management and a coordination point for programmers. Basic repositories may store data dictionary-type data design information, while more sophisticated ones may include application management and monitoring information.

- *Project management tools.* These typically support supervision of large-scale development, including monitoring, statistics, version control, and critical-path detection.

- *Test support.* This includes combining programs from multiple programmers, testing the result under various circumstances, and staging implementation on a production system.

When there is a need for large-scale C/S application development, such as development projects more than six months long, this could be a potential danger sign. One of the greatest advantages of C/S is that it breaks AD into smaller clients and several chunks, and uses more productive tools to produce those chunks, thus requiring fewer but more highly-skilled programmers. Large-scale C/S software development may indicate design failures, management failures or both.

Leveraged Scalability

When users plan data management around a "strategic" RDBMS, a C/S AD environment designed to use that RDBMS tends to out-perform and out-customize other alternatives. By making data management transparent to the programmer and taking advantage of RDBMS-specific data management optimizations, RDBMS-based C/S AD environments provide added value in many production systems.

New technologies for leveraging hardware and OS performance include multithreading, multiserver processing, and symmetric multiprocessing (SMP). These improve scalability – the ability of the server component of an application to serve multiple users. Some of these features are available in some DBMSs, some versions of UNIX, some network operating systems, and Microsoft Windows NT.

Several AD environments are also providing some of these features, notably multithreading. The Aberdeen Group states, however, most AD environments do not provide specific tools to parallelize code or transactions.

Flexibility

IS buyers should place a high value on AD environment flexibility because of the rapid pace of change in this technology, the multisupplier environment, and changing IS needs. The AD environment should be able to work in a variety of environments and adapt readily to software and hardware upgrades, organizational and strategic changes, and new end-user demands.

However, using a flexible AD environment often means paying a price in terms of reduced performance, reliability or increased complexity of administration. It also requires programmers to learn entirely new platforms and software environments.

According to the Aberdeen Group, a C/S AD environment should deliver flexibility by having:

- Open interoperability – applications produced with the environment should be interoperable with other applications, databases, and systems software;

- Multiarchitecture portability, including development on, and for the most popular platforms and RDBMSs; and

- Integration and customization capabilities, including repository-driven integration within the C/S AD environment, integration with data access tools to allow feedback between end-users and programmers, and the ability of programmers to customize the AD environment or its database of program code.

Software Lifecycle Support

Software Lifecycle Support (SLS) is something all C/S AD environments should offer. It includes support for the design, programming/testing, application deployment, and maintenance phases of the software lifecycle. (The software development lifecycle consists of planning, analysis, design, construction, testing, production and maintenance. Table 3.1 provides more detailed information about each stage.)

Table 3.1 The Software Development Lifecycle

Phase	Description	Function
1	Planning	(Or *requirements planning.*) Defining the broad requirements of the system and the methodology that will be used to build it
2	Analysis	(Or *systems analysis.*) Gathering information about the system from users and others who will be affected by its implementation and operation
3	Design	Codifying the information about the system into a model suitable for implementing on a computer, often using a defined systems design methodology
4	Construction	The coding of the information into a machine-readable format. This stage is the actual programming, or "code cutting"
5	Testing	Finding and fixing problems or "bugs," in the code
6	Production	The running of the system for the purpose for which it was intended
7	Maintenance	The continued fixing of bugs and alteration to the capabilities of the system, usually because of changing business requirements or suggestions for actual or perceived improvements

The Aberdeen Group states the most effective support includes not only the best in class tools for each stage of the lifecycle, but also integration of those tools. This is because the various stages of the software development lifecycle are concurrent to a great degree. Programming and testing will require constant redesign and reprogramming, for example.

Effective upper-CASE tools and C/S AD environments allow interruption of each tool at any stage, at any point, and feed changes backwards and forwards.

The Aberdeen Group recommends IS buyers should make it a point to look for C/S AD environments that:

- Offer strong tools for all stages of the software development lifecycle;
- Allow the programmer to move rapidly from stage to stage, starting at any point;

- Reflect changes at each stage, forward and backward; and

- Isolate input/output (I/O) data and program code so the programmer has the choice of dealing with them separately across stages or dealing with them together in one stage.

Lifecycle Elements That Should be Supported

Popular design tools fall into one of two areas: formalized "upper-CASE" application design tools such as TI's Information Engineering Facility (IEF), and database design tools such as those provided by RDBMS vendors such as Sybase and Oracle.

Generally, C/S AD environment vendors do not integrate either type of design tool into the AD process. They leave design to the DBMS or the developer.

Testing

C/S AD environment vendors provide testing tools similar to those included with 3GLs and 4GLs – mainly simple debuggers. Few tackle the problems of unit testing and integration testing for large-scale development.

Deployment

Increasingly, IS is looking at electronic software distribution. The increasing size and complexity of applications, and the need for frequent upgrades, make it uneconomical for IS to manually install software on users' computers.

Maintenance

Typical application maintenance tasks include performance monitoring, security, administration, backup and restore, recovery, audit trails, and accounting. Some of these services are provided by network operating systems and network computing architectures across a network, but C/S AD environments have generally not filled in the gaps. Repositories would be a potentially effective mechanism for logging and administering C/S applications.

Programmer-productivity Technologies

Do not expect too much from programmer-productivity technologies; in particular cases, they can produce major gains, but they have rarely achieved continuous measurable improvements over an entire organization for an extended period of time. There are two main reasons for this.

First, these technologies require a cultural change from programmers and the IS department. They demand different ways of thinking about the software development process and shift the balance of power between programmer and supervisor. They render obsolete techniques which the company's most outstanding programmers have used to achieve their edge.

Second, these technologies have a narrow focus. They restrict programming to empower certain types of programming. It is very much like concentrating on exercising one part of the body, such as the arms, and ignoring the rest, to get strong arms. The result will be strong arms, but the rest of the body will be relatively weak.

The Aberdeen Group finds three programmer-productivity technologies especially promising when combined with a C/S AD environment. These are:

- Scripting languages;
- Visual programming environments (VPEs); and
- Object-oriented programming.

Scripting Languages

Scripting languages are an evolution of 4GLs which allow programmers to code GUI applications as a set of "scripts" triggered by end-user actions. In other words, it is event-driven programming.

Visual Programming Environments

VPEs are usually used to enhance the presentation component of a C/S application. They display programming tools in GUI terms and allow the programmer to paint GUI screens with point-and-click commands.

VPE-style development focuses on making the interface user-friendly. Also, a VPE can generate large amounts of basic GUI code which can be reused.

IS should consider a VPE a key element in C/S AD environments because it aids users in customizing increasingly popular GUIs, such as Microsoft Windows. Either alone or in combination with scripting languages, VPEs can sharply increase programmer productivity.

Object-oriented Programming

This technology is applicable to all parts of a C/S application. It can yield major improvements in programmer productivity in some situations.

The Aberdeen Group states fragmentary studies show an average improvement in development of about 35% after a year or more spent in learning OOP. However, if implemented on a large scale, OOP can be a massive technical change for programmers and the IS department, which will require major retraining costs and may meet with significant resistance.

Most so-called object-oriented environments available today offer watered-down versions of OOP. These versions allow programmers to include as little or as much "real" OOP as seems appropriate. The resulting compromise can be more complicated than using either OOP or a traditional language.

The complexity of the move to OOP means most organizations should not try for massive conversions of existing programs; instead, they should consider bringing OOP technology in only as an adjunct to a VPE.

Support for Other Software Development Technologies

Technologies that may be of special value to the enterprise include open transaction processing (TP), APIs, toolkits, multimedia (including imaging), and workflow/electronic mail-enabling.

A large number of user applications have been written using IBM's Customer Information Control System (CICS) TP monitor toolkit. These are usually for high-performance, high-bandwidth TP on System/390 mainframes.

An open TP monitor API is based on standards for TP monitors, such as the X/Open Corp.'s XA standard and the Open Systems International (OSI)-distributed TP standard. Open-TP monitors are relatively new to the market. In a typical OLTP environment, they mesh two or more C/S DBMSs from different suppliers.

The advent of open TP monitors and the porting of CICS to low-end platforms such as IBM's RS/6000 means programmers can write server components of

C/S programs for multiple platforms and suppliers. Also, this allows legacy applications based on these TP monitors be to ported to C/S networks with relative ease.

Looking to the Future

In assessing C/S AD environments, IS buyers look not only at product features currently available, but also at the rapidity and focus of the vendor's technology development. Users looking at the future of AD environments should focus on two areas: distributed program development and business modeling.

Distributed Program Development

Ultimately, the developer/administrator of a C/S application wants to view it both as a whole, as if it were running on one computer, and in its separate client, server, and communications parts.

This dual view is not offered by C/S AD environments today. However, as vendors of AD environments automate the development process, they will incorporate dual-view technology to the point where implementing a C/S application will be almost as easy as implementing a single-system one.

The key to this will be a repository that stores a variety of data about applications under development and in production. Vendors who use a repository to drive their toolsets will probably have an advantage in developing dual-view technology.

Business Modeling

Creating business models through an OOP-based repository in a C/S AD environment is an important step in scaling business process reengineering or establishing electronic customer links to enterprise-class applications.

By embedding enterprise considerations, such as "seek follow-up sales of related products," in a reusable class library, with reusable business rules and business objects, IS will simplify development of large-scale applications. Previously, developers of these applications were required to re-code business-specific logic for each new application or upgrade.

OOP is most suited for such business model design. OOP-based software is far more modular, capable of representing business concepts, portable, and

---

interoperable than legacy software. Companies that have developed OOP-based business models find that changing the model to reflect changing company structures and strategies is relatively straightforward.

Chapter 4

Application Development, Part II

Considerations When Developing Applications

Several factors must be taken into consideration when applications are being developed. First, the composition of the development team must be examined. Initially, business workgroups were seen as the solution, but over time, their lack of computing disciplines led to break-down-prone applications. The applications could not be patched or restored because no one had kept a log of the development cycle or the code or because some members had left the organization. Some applications did not integrate or exchange data with other applications in the organization or were so specialized they had to be entirely rewritten when the organization began to establish an enterprisewide C/S system. MIS must work out the best composition for a development team.

Workgroup Development Teams

One of the reasons C/S became popular in business was because it broke the hold of MIS over the corporation. Users tended to know the business best and could best state their requirements. Given sophisticated tools, they could build applications which would be patterned after the way they work, rather than adapting to applications built by programmers, which were developed for coding clarity and programming ease.

However, the workgroup route to AD in C/S is fraught with pitfalls. Developing applications in this environment is more difficult than on the mainframe because it is very complex – there are more, different types of computers attached to many different networks, sometimes using different topologies.

Developers must understand the components of the computers and the networks in the corporate system. They must understand how networks work and understand how the applications they are building interact with the operating systems on which they will be run. This is a full-time task for professionals, and it will be very difficult for business users to master these complexities on top of their existing jobs.

Problems with Using Workgroups for Development

In addition to having little time to master the complexities of the corporation's computer environment, workgroups of business users are not trained programmers, so they miss out on a lot of essentials. The basic housekeeping chores or tasks taken for granted in the mainframe world – data security, data integrity, network security, the idea of backup and recovery, testing, and quality assurance (QA) – are not performed because the members of workgroups lack the training mainframe programmers have received.

There is a normal pattern of AD in distributed workgroups. A workgroup buys computers, creates an application, and links the computers together. Then, the system breaks down because the application needs enhancement, there is a bug to be repaired or there are network problems.

Individual business department workers are not equipped to handle ongoing maintenance, and they must turn to the MIS department for help. These are all problems which have existed in the mainframe environment and have been dealt with there for years.

Scalability is another problem. Generally, workgroups build applications for less than 50 users in order to deal with tactical problems. As a result, they do not ensure the applications are reusable or can be scaled up to run on an enterprisewide network. Further, because workgroups tend to develop applications on their own, without reference to what other workgroups in the corporation are doing, the corporation often ends up with many different applications which cannot communicate.

In short, workgroups do not step back and examine the bigger picture. This is partly because they are composed of business users who have now added a new discipline – AD – to their duties. It is also partly because the members of workgroups do not have the training in computer science to be able to step back and know what to search for in the bigger picture.

Further, the composition of workgroups changes as people leave a corporation or are transferred. Once the system breaks down or is shown to be full of bugs, it is difficult to repair because the people who built the application may not have documented their work or have left the organization.

Finally, the role of the client in the environment may be continually changing, and members of workgroups developing applications may not be able to take time off from their normal duties to rewrite the applications they have developed.

Creating the Right Development Team

One solution to the problems of using business workgroups to develop applications is to ensure the AD team blends people with expertise in different areas. For example, it could have people with PC expertise in the area of application building, someone from central MIS with expertise in the classical disciplines – concurrency, integrity, security, and multiuser requirements. Such teams should not be permanent, but should be assembled as they are needed for a project.

Also, instead of taking on a whole project, developers should adopt the Cartesian method and separate it into smaller, more manageable pieces. They can learn from each of these smaller projects as they are completed.

For example, the first step into AD in C/S could be restricted to empowering end-users and knowledge workers with Decision Support System (DSS) or Executive Information Service (EIS) tools. These would be read-only, and MIS must ensure it has a manageable and quantifiable requirement to store and package data. Meanwhile, end-users would become comfortable with working in a graphical PC-based environment. See Figures 4.1 and 4.2.

Figure 4.1 What Developers Look for in Client/Server Applications

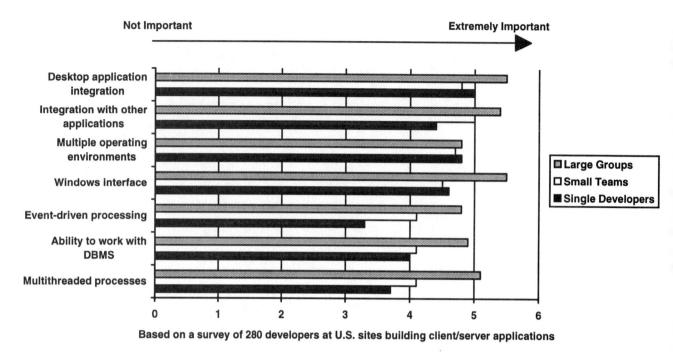

Based on a survey of 280 developers at U.S. sites building client/server applications

Source: International Data Corp./Informationweek

Figure 4.2 Development Priorities

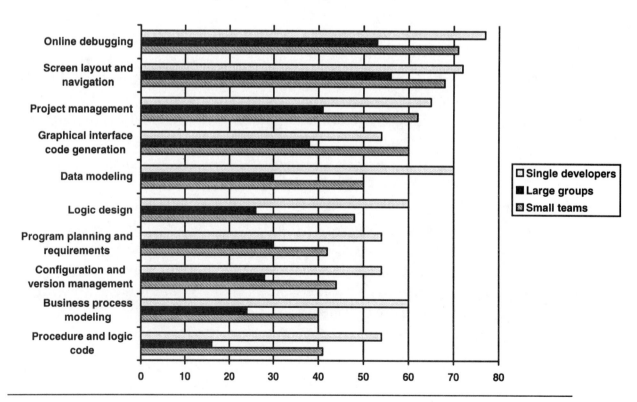

Some Methodologies for Application Development

There are various methodologies for AD, each with its own adherent qualities. Occasionally, one methodology or another becomes popular – structured systems analysis and design method (SSADM) in the 1980s, rapid application development (RAD) in the 1990s. The most important factor is: the methodology used must match corporate requirements, the skillsets of the development teams, and the technologies and tools the corporation will buy for AD.

Waterfall versus Rapid Application Development

For years, the standard method of AD has been the "waterfall" method – developers use a syntactical language and take a step-by-step approach. They finish one step before beginning the next. Each phase must be completed in an orderly, serial fashion. User requirements are analyzed; then the application is designed, coded, tested, and deployed.

One of the problems with this approach: it is very error-prone because testing comes at almost the very end. This positions the development team for a potential disaster.

Another problem: this approach assumes user needs can be identified accurately by drawing written specifications for users to examine. However, in today's fast-changing business world, it cannot be assumed that user needs will remain the same over the span of a year or more. As the corporation's needs change, users' needs will change with them. Further, users can only analyze what is in front of them; few will be knowledgeable enough to point out what has been left out or take the trouble to do so.

This has led to the adoption of RAD methodology. In short, RAD allows developers to build a prototype within a few days, bring it back to users for validation, and then go on to build the next stage. This is called the whirlpool method.

The basic concept of the RAD approach is iterative development using rapid prototyping tools and less time spent on early analysis and design. There are dangers to this, of course; if planning is reduced too sharply or cut out altogether, the chances of the development team making a disastrous error are as great as if they had gone back to the waterfall method.

What is the solution? Learn to balance traditional analytical skills with the more spontaneous RAD approach. The development team must still identify the initial business requirements. However, instead of then drawing written specifications for users to review, the team would begin prototyping the application. Ultimately, the rapid prototyping will help the development team design better systems, because it will begin discovering new kinds of interactions among the data and other new functions it would not have thought of otherwise.

RAD tools make it easy to change applications during the development process so lengthy analysis is not as important as in the waterfall method. The interface can be created first, and can be changed quickly; the data structure can be added later. In the waterfall method, a mistake in the interface could mean redesigning underlying data structures.

To teach mainframe programmers to adjust to new RAD tools:

- Identify specifications for the first 10 or 12 tables, getting a good idea of how they fit together;

- Let programmers naturally discover additional data requirements as they are building the user interface; and

- Have a sense of the basic database requirements. Ensure the data is normalized, there are no data redundancies, data protection and validation have been considered, and the big picture – the system's goal and its impact on the overall information enterprise – has been considered.

The Three-Tier Development Approach

As users increasingly adopt mobile devices – personal digital assistants (PDAs), pagers, telephones, personal communicators, and smart cards – the traditional two-tier approach to C/S AD becomes outdated. Developers must design systems so client machines can be easily pulled away from their servers with no loss of business efficiency.

The answer to this problem is to adopt a three-tier approach to C/S AD. This consists of a presentation or user interface, a "function" or method for delivering information to the interface, and the actual data. The presentation part of this model can exist on a worker's PC, a PDA with dial-up capabilities or a touch-tone analog or cellular telephone.

Developers must rethink their concept of data. The data layer will become both the information and its location – on a relational database server, a mainframe, a minicomputer, a UNIX workstation or a PC.

The idea is the client need not be tied to any one software package. If this can be achieved, one application can be used for every type of remote client a company uses.

To enable this, the middle layer – the functional layer or method for delivering information to the interface – must be redefined. Most businesses see this layer as the actual software application, but the Gartner Group has expanded it to include middleware and communications.

The Gartner Group asserts intelligent messaging agents must sit on every computing resource and pass containers of messages, data, transactions or instructions between a client machine and a middle-layer server, which will do most of the application processing.

Application Development Standards: the Corporate Application Programming Interface

Centralized application cannot satisfy today's business needs, which are delivery speed, sensitivity to business needs, and aggressive competition. While host-centric development cannot meet these needs, going to the other extreme – implementing a fully decentralized AD approach – has its own problems including wasted effort through redundant development, lack of information sharing across the corporation, and a lack of industrial-strength applications.

Market research firm Forrester Research, Inc., based in Cambridge, Massachusetts, believes the solution is to employ a new model for software development which it calls the Corporate API. This will enable decentralization while allowing the corporation to retain control.

In the Corporate API model, the MIS staff is divided between central MIS and line MIS. Central MIS will remain in the MIS department, while line MIS staffers will be moved out to business departments. Both central and line MIS will be separate, autonomous groups with different tasks and different agendas. Central MIS will build computing utilities – the "mortar" in the corporate computer system. These utilities will allow information sharing, application integration, and data access across systems built by line MIS. They will include components such as the networking hardware, protocols, and software.

Figure 4.3 The Corporate Application Programming Interface

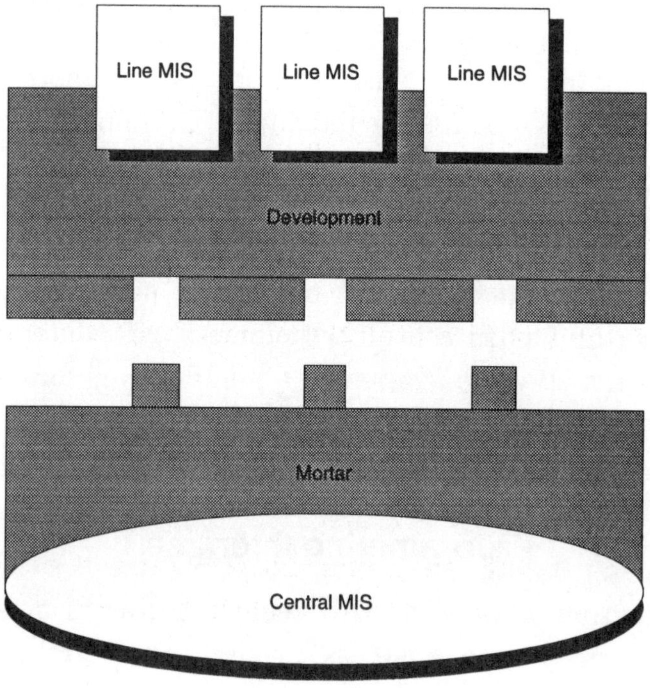

Line MIS will have full responsibility for AD. It can focus on creating high-value applications quickly and efficiently because it will be shielded from low-level technical details by the technology mortar created by central MIS. See Figure 4.3.

Central Management Information Systems Responsibilities

Central MIS must ensure it builds and manages the mortar layer, which is the foundation for all distributed corporate applications. This will prevent separate business units from going their own way and duplicating each others' work. Central MIS has five responsibilities:

1. *Network backbone.*

2. *Navigational technology.* This includes naming, directory, and security services.

3. *Messaging.* This ranges from basic electronic mail (E-mail) to object request brokers for linking distributed applications.

4. *Information repositories.* These are databases designed for sharing data and AD information. Although most of the information will be created in the business units by line MIS, it is the duty of central MIS to create and manage the repositories.

5. *Legacy systems.* These will continue to be the responsibility of central MIS, which must provide facilities that allow new applications to interact with legacy systems.

Line Management Information Systems Responsibilities

The work done by central MIS is designed to make the development task of line MIS easier by hiding the complexity of the corporate computing environment. The charter of line MIS is fast delivery of business-critical applications.

The Corporate API allows line MIS to easily access corporate data and resources throughout the technology "mortar" developed by central MIS, choose development tools which fit its needs, and share value across the corporation through common data and development repositories.

Line MIS has five core tasks in development:

1. *Selecting development tools.* Tools picked must match developers' skills and the corporation's business needs. They must also exploit the information-sharing capabilities of the corporate API – which means that, if

central MIS has not done its job properly, line MIS will be restricted to using outdated tools.

2. *Choosing development methodologies.*

3. *Setting data definitions.* Line MIS must supply business-driven data definitions to central MIS.

4. *Managing distributed systems.* It is the duty of line MIS to administer the systems it builds.

5. *Enforcing quality control.*

Figure 4.4 illustrates the division of labor between line MIS and central MIS.

Figure 4.4 Division of Labor under the Corporate Application Programming Interface

Line MIS:

Line MIS builds line of business applications and cross-function systems...

Central MIS:

Central MIS builds mortar to hide technical complexity...

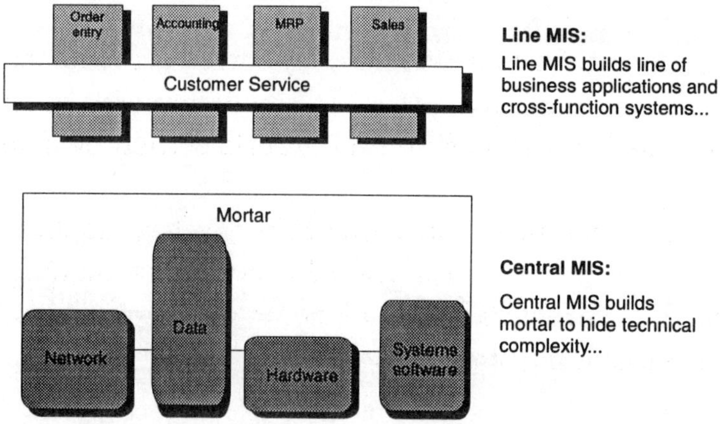

Source: Forrester Research, Inc.

Adopting the Corporate Application Programming Interface

Corporations must take two actions to adopt the corporate API model: first, they must divide technical responsibilities between central MIS and line MIS. Second, they must draft an agreement between the two.

This agreement will define the following:

- *Who does what?* It will lay out how work will be divided between central MIS and line MIS. To eliminate redundancy, the two will share each other's work on a technology level through agreed-upon interfaces.

- *Who is in charge?* Corporate and line MIS will be separate, autonomous groups. The agreement will define how conflict between the two will be resolved.

- *Who pays the bill?* The contract must specify how technology acquisition and development will be funded.

- *What is the plan?* This will set the technical agenda for the enterprise. Central MIS and line MIS must work together to decide what new products will be adopted and at what rate this will be done.

The corporate API contract will be developed by senior management at central MIS, line MIS, and the business units. This will prevent executives from overruling the agreement in the short-term interests of their own departments.

These representatives must also ensure line MIS develops applications within the guidelines laid down in the corporate API, develop a binding system for resolving disputes, and develop a mechanism for dealing with whatever falls between the cracks – including staff and applications.

Implementing the Corporate Application Programming Interface

Forrester Research, Inc. recommends companies adopt a three-phase approach to implementing the corporate API. These phases are embarking, transitioning, and discovery.

Embarking

Large companies will begin moving away from the old centralized structure. The focus will then be on shifting developers out to the business units. Line MIS begins moving down the C/S learning curve by working on simple decision support systems, while central MIS is restructured to build the computing "mortar," starting with the corporate network.

The corporations will have to:

- *Build senior management support* for the corporate API.

- *Staff line MIS.* Forrester Research, Inc. believes the best way to do this is to get a combination of power users and LAN administrators from the business unit, and leading developers from the old glass house.

- *Refocus central MIS.* Central MIS will be reorganized into four groups: legacy systems, network and navigational services, messaging and information repository facilities, and "mortar marketing." These will educate line MIS on the benefits of the corporate API.

Transitioning

In this phase, central MIS has recast itself as a service provider to line MIS. However, it will still be responsible for maintaining the remaining legacy applications. Meanwhile, line MIS has completed its first high-impact applications which leverage the mortar services, and business units are beginning to see the fruits of the corporate API – faster development of the right applications.

This is what is needed to take the corporate API to the transition level:

- Central MIS must showcase early "mortar" victories.

- Line MIS must master complex system development.

- The steering committee will have to take on two new tasks: providing a forum for line MIS representatives to critique and guide the work of central MIS, and establishing an arbitration board to resolve arguments between line and central MIS.

Discovery

The scope of the mortar provided by central MIS and the applications developed by line MIS will extend to customers and suppliers. The interaction between central and line MIS will be fine-tuned. Companies will have to:

- Change the mortar at two levels. First, with the availability of object request brokers (ORBs) and products based on standards, such as the Open

Software Foundation's (OSF's) Distributed Computing Environment (DCE), corporations can take a more architectural approach. Second, this system's infrastructure will be pushed out to customers and suppliers, to support the workflow and customer service initiatives of line MIS.

- Push separate line MIS groups to work together.
- Put the final element of the steering committee – the business and technology planning forum – into place.

Figure 4.5 illustrates the organization of the corporate API.

Figure 4.5 Organizing for the Corporate Application Programming Interface

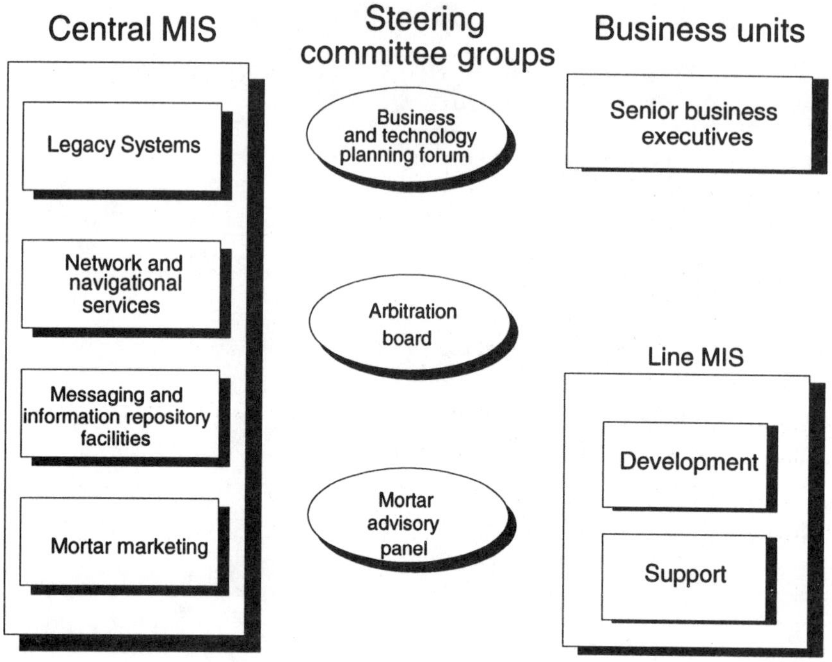

Central MIS | Steering committee groups | Business units

- Legacy Systems
- Network and navigational services
- Messaging and information repository facilities
- Mortar marketing

- Business and technology planning forum
- Arbitration board
- Mortar advisory panel

- Senior business executives

Line MIS
- Development
- Support

Source: Forrester Research, Inc.

Imposing Standards

At the next level down from the corporate API is the imposition of standards. While standards should be imposed for both software and hardware, this section will deal with software standards because hardware standards fall outside the scope of this report.

Imposing standards makes life easier by reducing support and training costs and simplifying integration. Many corporations believe that C/S will force them to implement new software standards. Tackling the standards issue is a two-phase process, in Forrester Research, Inc.'s view. Corporations must get out in front of the curve by looking ahead, then adjust for the long term.

Figure 4.6 shows some of the benefits of imposing software standards.

Figure 4.6 What Are the Benefits of Software Standards?

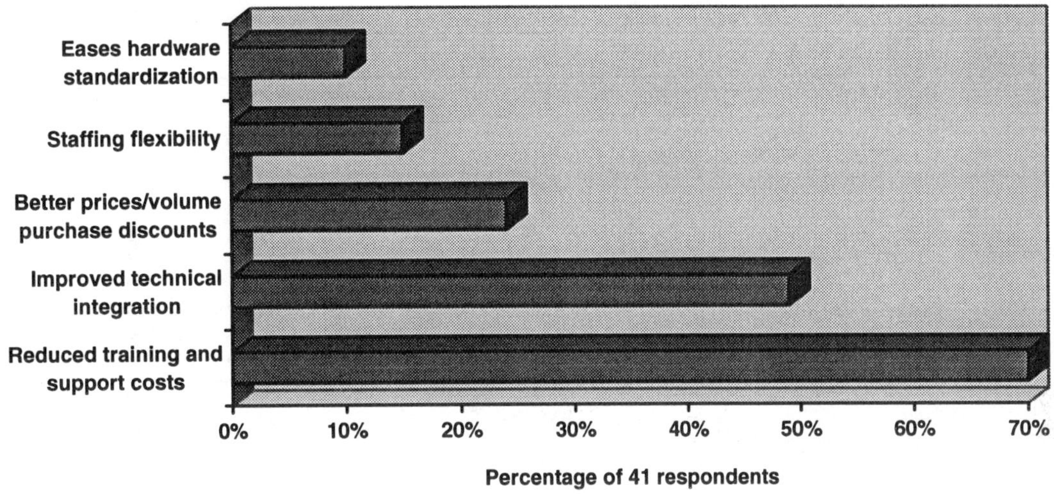

Percentage of 41 respondents

Source: Forrester Research, Inc.

Getting out in Front of the Curve

Large companies must make decisions in four key areas of distributed computing software: infrastructure technology, server databases, development tools, and personal productivity applications. The tasks will be divided between central MIS and line MIS.

- Infrastructure will be a top priority for central MIS as it prepares the mortar for the corporate API. Adhering to the standards set by central MIS should be non-negotiable.

- *Server databases* will be a key issue for line MIS. New profit-making applications, built by line MIS, depend on server databases, such as Informix, Oracle, and Sybase. As these applications increase in number and importance, line MIS will have to select one database engine to ease integration and support.

- *C/S development tools* will be the second-tier concern for line MIS. It is more important to make the database choice first, for three reasons: AD is localized and tactical, the price wars among tool vendors make it economically feasible to try out several products before making a decision, and the leading tools support all the popular server databases.

- *Personal productivity applications* – this field is a low priority for central MIS. Instead of trying to revamp the installed base of desktop applications, it would make more sense for central MIS to rationalize new desktop software purchases. The decisions must consider the needs of the business units and the developing infrastructure constraints and should not be based solely on economics.

Adjusting for the Long Term

Once the development organization has been restructured around the corporate API, central MIS will clamp down on infrastructure and desktop standards. It will then consider helping line MIS (and users) link up to the central plumbing and investigate new technology. Next, line and central MIS will collaborate on database decisions. Line MIS will own the server databases used for local applications and central MIS will handle the administration of centralized data. Development tools will top the priority list of line MIS. Now that line MIS is building mission-critical applications, it must standardize on tools to build robust applications within the corporate API and facilitate code reuse and programmer mobility.

Chapter 5

Application Development, Part III

Building C/S systems takes a great deal of hard work. Here are some actual examples of company efforts to design and implement C/S systems.

SQL Statements Can Kill

At a process manufacturing company, common business-oriented language (COBOL) programmers were given the task of writing embedded SQL statements against an Oracle RDBMS back-end.

By the time the programmers were finished, they had put the SQL statements is such a state of disarray that one backup job took 22 hours, said Cheryl Currid, president of Houston, Texas-based consulting firm, Currid & Co. After a couple of weeks of trying to resolve the problem, the programmers gave up and hired an SQL expert, who unscrambled their SQL statements and reduced processing time to less than an hour.

Data Synchronization Can be a Pain

A pilot C/S project launched to move financial data off the mainframe onto OS/2 servers at international hotel chain Holiday Inns Worldwide, based in

Atlanta, Georgia, was a big success – but the chain decided against a full implementation because changes made to accounts on the corporation's IBM 3090 host mainframe were not being picked up by the servers.

IS staff were forced to fax changes back and forth, enter them manually at the servers or repeat the data download on the mainframe. The chain was using Version 1.0 of Dun & Bradstreet Software's SmartStream package.

Pilot Projects May Not Scale up

Looking before leaping is a good thing, especially when implementing C/S. Experts say corporations going to C/S should start with a small, pilot project and learn as they go along.

This approach does not always work as well as it should. According to Brent Williams, an analyst at Framingham, Massachusetts-based market research firm International Data Corp., many C/S projects fail because the pilots were too limited. For example, a 10-screen prototype is tested with five occasional users and works well, so it is expanded to a 50-screen application and is rolled out to 200 users in production.

At this point, performance issues become important with the database because the developers spent so much time on building the GUIs and SQL statements, they ignore the data modeling and data integrity functions, Williams says. The moral of this tale? Look twice before leaping into C/S: once at the beginning of the pilot project, and again at its conclusion.

Ensure Screen Element Compatibility

There is such a phenomenon as too much of a good thing, as some developers using sophisticated tools such as Powersoft's PowerBuilder have discovered. PowerBuilder allows users to build very complex GUIs with pull-down and pop-up menus, color, and graphics.

These sophisticated tools offer so many functions developers can wind up building GUIs with incompatible screen elements for functions such as adding a new entry, removing, deleting, and closing a window, and exiting and quitting the application.

IS has to globally define many of the windows functions and their appearance. This saves time and effort, and by ensuring reusability, saves money.

Empowerment Can Backfire

The battle cry of many C/S proponents is "empowering the end-user" – a phrase with a nice ring to it. It has undertones of democracy, and somewhere in the dim recesses of users' minds, revives memories of the downtrodden masses fighting for their freedom.

Of course, few remember what happens when the downtrodden masses do battle – there is chaos. Chaos is often the result when developers build too much freedom for the end-user into an application.

Consider Technology Investment Strategies Corp. (Framingham, Massachusetts), for example. The firm's workgroup and end-user computing department built a C/S application using SQL Server without realizing what they had done, and after users had made changes to data views, the administrator would have to assign new access privileges so that the users could have access to the changes. The reason for this is that, when a user group made changes to a particular view, the old view was deleted, and no one had permission to access the new one.

The Version Control Blues

Most large projects are delivered in stages. This makes sense – rolling a project out all at once is technically and economically unfeasible and will leave the corporation without its system.

The trouble is, when a project is being rolled out in stages, different user groups may have different versions of an application, and this can cause problems with security and data synchronization.

The St. Louis, Missouri-based brokerage firm, Edward D. Jones & Co., discovered this situation while converting more than 2,400 branch offices from IBM mainframes to C/S systems. This was done to improve response time, so brokers in each office could get more up-to-date pricing data.

The firm decided to replace its IBM Series 1 front-end processors with an IBM RS/6000, and retro-fit its satellite data network to run TCP/IP and Ethernet.

However, because some C/S products were in early, non-robust stages, changes were needed in operating systems or applications.

Updating to a new version of software or applying a bug fix to all clients or servers was an enormous task. Concerns with security and data synchronization forced the firm to temporarily postpone its selection of an RDBMS, client and server hardware platforms, and OS.

The solution to the problem of version control and synchronization is to purchase one of the electronic software distribution packages now available on the market or to get Microsoft's System Management Server (SMS, formerly called Hermes), which has built-in electronic software distribution capabilities.

Chapter 6

Middleware

Overview

Once the front-end of an application is separated from the back-end, which is what happens in C/S, middleware becomes essential. The system needs some type of mechanism to coordinate communications between the GUI front-end (the client) and the back-end (the server), especially if they are on different computers.

In general, middleware products handle the communications chores involved in distributed applications. These include translations among different operating systems and networking environments. Middleware products also provide management services to ensure that queries and responses arrive at their destination.

This can save a large amount of money, especially for corporations that are downsizing or distributing applications; a recent IBM survey showed that 20% to 40% of the cost of developing application code is accounted for by the code that handles communications.

How Middleware Works

Each middleware product has four major components – a call analyzer, a global directory, a translator, and a response manager. When the application calls for data using the API, the middleware will locate the data being called by consulting the global directory. If the data called is no longer there, the call will be passed to the response manager, which provides an appropriate response. If the call is valid, it is passed to the translator, which translates it

---

into a form corresponding to the API of the target data store. The target database responds, and the response manager passes the reply back to the application (see Figure 6.1).

Figure 6.1 The Position of Middleware

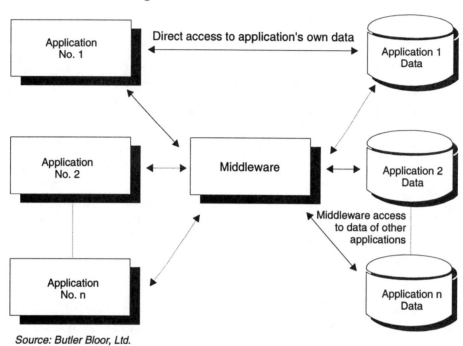

Source: Butler Bloor, Ltd.

Message-oriented Middleware versus Remote Procedure Calls

RPCs are used to synchronize the processes of clients and servers in a C/S environment and are a form of middleware. An RPC is a call to a procedure or application on remote hardware. Message-oriented middleware can be used in its place. Unlike RPCs, message-oriented middleware allows concurrent processing. This is because the middleware has a queued messaging function.

The queued messaging function allows an application to send a request or a file to another application across the enterprise, then perform another task while waiting for a response.

State Street Bank of Quincy, Massachusetts has been using EZ-Bridge Transact, a message-oriented middleware package from Systems Strategies, Inc., to interconnect applications running on computers from Tandem

Computers, Inc., IBM, Digital Equipment Corp. (DEC) and UNIX systems. EZ-Bridge Transact was selected because it guarantees message delivery. It has also cut development times for complex applications from several months to several weeks.

Messaging and queuing frees application developers from worrying about telecommunications links. Concurrent engineering and financial environments, where a single customer query may require information from several applications on different systems, are ideal for message-oriented applications.

There is currently a proposed standard for interfacing applications to message-oriented middleware, called Message Queue Interface (MQI) from IBM. Meanwhile, several vendors have formed the Message-oriented Middleware consortium. They are Horizon Strategies, Inc.; DEC; Momentum Software Corp.; PeerLogic, Inc.; Systems Strategies, Inc.; and Covia Technologies.

Chapter 7

Testing, Metrics, and Quality

Overview

Testing is perhaps the most important aspect of application development. Unless an application is tested thoroughly, there is no way of knowing whether or not it will fail at a crucial moment. Testing supports the development process, and corporations can only build their applications as quickly as they can thoroughly test them. It is not possible to build an application and expect it to hold up without testing it thoroughly.

One of the most important aspects of testing is planning. First, testers have to decide what the scope of the test is going to be. Only the largest corporations can afford the expense, manpower, and time needed to exercise every single iteration of a program. For most organizations, it makes more financial sense to test for the most important factors, and what the most important factors are will depend on what the application was designed to do.

Before beginning the actual test, testers have to determine the probability of memory errors. With DOS applications, memory problems would present themselves fairly quickly, because an application was constrained by the 640K-byte DOS limitation. GUI operating systems are playing with more memory, and they are sophisticated in their handling of memory usage and module swapping. The same memory problem that caused an early problem in a DOS application may take many cycles to emerge in the more sophisticated and powerful GUI operating environment.

The way to resolve these problems is to design and implement a properly detailed and thorough test plan.

Know What to Test

Attempting to test every iteration of an application is pointless; few corporations have the time, money or manpower to even attempt this. Nor will gathering that information help to identify where the application is weak and where it is strong.

The key in testing is to know what to test. One approach is to apply the Pareto Principle – better known as the 80/20 rule: 80% of an application's work is done by 20% of the code so test that 20% of the code thoroughly.

Another approach is to know everything about how an application works. The testers want to discern how it processes data, how it interacts with RPCs and other commands, and in some cases, what every line of code does.

Yet another approach is to examine the input and the output, ensure the output is what is required for a given input, and leave it at that. This is called the black box method.

Types of Tests

Stress Testing

This method, where an application is tested repeatedly until it breaks down, is one which is sometimes used more often than it should be. Remember that a whole battery of tests must be conducted in order to ensure an application is working properly.

Functional Testing

Functional testing answers the question of whether the application is interacting properly with the user. It also determines if an application produces the expected output.

Black Box Testing

Black box testing is a concept taken from systems analysis. The key here is that it is not important to know how things work "inside" the black box; the important thing is the input and output. Black box testing attempts to answer the question, "Do I get back what I expect when I insert something?"

Acceptability Testing

Acceptability testing answers the question, "Does the application meet the needs of the members of the business community?" This is very important because if an application is not accepted by the end-users or the business community, it might need to be re-worked.

Regression Testing

Regression testing is performed after functional enhancements or maintenance repairs are made to a program to determine whether changes have introduced errors. It is a very time-consuming and tedious process and most development organizations only use regression testing after major enhancements or repairs have been made. However, even minor changes can introduce errors so regression testing is necessary. Because of its tedious, time-consuming nature, regression testing is a prime candidate for automation.

Other Forms of Testing

Other forms of testing include function points analysis, code point coverage, and mean time between failures (MTBF). The most important question to be answered, however, is a simple one: does the application do what the user wants it to do? Merely examining the metrics will not give a usable answer.

Questions Testers Should Ask Themselves

As they begin the testing process, there are several questions that testers should ask themselves.

- Does the application work? Does it look right? If menus, dialog boxes, and windows are not where they are supposed to be or do not look the way they are should, there is a problem.

- Is the generated data correct? To confirm this, there are different ways to reach an application's data. Bitmap comparison is a partial solution because the bitmap validation process is unwieldy and time- and space-consuming, and also may present an incomplete picture of what is actually happening.

- How does the application handle concurrent requests, security, and lockouts? The best, indeed the only, way to test this is through automation.

- What is the impact on systems resources? Repeated running of an application may have subtle effects on underlying systems resources that add up, over time, and cause major problems. A testing tool must be able to report and evaluate the state of the application at any given moment in time. This involves more than checking on systems resources. The testing tool must be able to drive an application long enough and hard enough to determine when it begins to affect local memory and when it begins to affect systems resources on the server.

- Does the application give the performance levels required? It may work well, look good, have all the right answers, have minimum impact on systems resources, and still not achieve the performance levels.

Approaches to Testing

The two major approaches to testing are record/playback and programmatic testing.

Record/playback allows testers to swiftly capture all user interactions with an application and replay them whenever a test is run. They are relatively inexpensive and allow non-technical staff to build libraries of automated test cases. They are easy to use and are relatively inexpensive.

The disadvantage of record/playback is its sensitivity to changes in the user interface, which can occur fairly rapidly and radically. Also, record/playback tapes are difficult to edit, even when they are translated into ASCII mode.

Record/playback is also known as capture/playback. This method can be very useful in certain situations. At the USA Group, Inc., in Fishers, Indiana, it is being used during AD and system maintenance to find bugs.

The USA Group has two large multiple virtual storage (MVS) applications – one for student loan guarantees, and the other for student loan servicing. These are written in COBOL and Application Development System (ADS)/Online, using the integrated data management system (IDMS) database from Cullinet Software, Inc., which was brought over by Computer Associates International, Inc. some years ago.

There is almost no debugging environment for ADS/Online, so test cases had to be constructed, executed, and re-executed with test databases rebuilt each time. The USA Group purchased CICS Playback from Compuware Corp. of Farmington Hills, Michigan to run its tests.

CICS Playback was designed especially for large applications, which are difficult to rigorously test for production conditions before system implementation. It performs the following tests:

- Builds realistic test cases by capturing actual transactions, related database, and file activity;

- Executes repeatable tests in a simulated production environment, which makes it unnecessary to re-key transactions and restore test databases between tests;

- Aids analysis of test results by flagging all screen and database differences; and

- Documents test results.

Although it was designed to help test online mainframe applications, CICS Playback can be used for other purposes. For example, it can capture and maintain user scripts for establishing a database or defining a printer. CICS Playback can be run in an unattended mode or can be set to run interactively. The unattended mode is best for long tests with high transaction rates. When run interactively, CICS Playback allows testers to change transaction input and view output before moving to the next transaction.

The USA Group uses CICS Playback to save test cases so that, whenever a program goes from production back to testing, the same tests can be run again and their results compared to previous results. Playback has helped cut total testing time by about 50%.

The programmatic approach to testing typically offers testers greater control over automation of their test cases and the ability to create very complex and robust test suites. The advantages of programmatic testing are the power, flexibility, and reusability of a well-programmed set of test cases; the disadvantages are the initial investment required to program and the requirement that a tester be knowledgeable about programming.

Simplicity is the Key

The actual tests themselves should be kept simple, whether manual or automated. When complex test cases appear, chances are the testers have not done enough planning in advance and are trying to compensate for this.

Often, poorly planned tests result in redundancy. It is also important to plan the test matrices. If the matrices become too complex, testers can create a control log similar to a table that maps their test cases to their functional matrices. It summarizes things so testers can easily see the test coverage.

Designing Test Cases

There are certain principles involved in designing test cases which will help testing run smoothly.

Test Case Independence

One of the principles in designing a test case is independence. The current test case should not depend on the success of the previous test case in order to run successfully. If Test Case 10 fails to execute, for example, Test Case 11 should still be able to run properly.

Each test case should be self-contained. Each test case needs data requirements, and these requirements must be built-in to the baseline database. The test team should be able to archive from the baseline databases.

A baseline database contains data the test cases require. If, for example, the test case expects to have data on adding three new users to the system, that data should be in the baseline database. For example, Test Case A will try to do the addition. It will also verify whether the addition worked correctly. Test Case B may also look at adding three users, but to different departments in the corporation. It might also look at something else to do with the three users. Because the test team wants to be able to run Test Case B even if Test Case A fails, it will have in the baseline database a model with the same data that Test Case A had, but with a different number on it.

Archiving from the baseline databases requires a large amount of planning because it is common to have 10, 12 or even 15 baseline databases (some of which will be very common).

Defining baseline databases is not difficult. The test team goes through a process of building test cases based on, for example, a user point of view, and asks itself what the requirements of that business user are. If the requirement is to add a new user, the test team must ensure a record exists which the test case can use. The baseline database is restored before each test cycle.

One of the benefits of test case independence is that it leads to defining the size of the test case.

Home Base

The concept of home base is simple: all test cases should start at the same point in the application. If a test team is running Test Case 10 and it fails, and the team then wants to run Test Case 11, the test must know where it is in the application.

This is not what usually happens. In most instances, when a test case fails, the test team does not know where it is in the application. If all test cases start at the same place, for example, at the first screen in the application, it is much simpler, because when one case fails, the next simply goes to the first screen automatically. Many of the newer testing tools offer this facility.

No Gap, No Overlap

When designing a test case, the test team must build a test matrix to show its coverage analysis. All the business functions should be listed in the matrix.

The test team must ensure every business function is in the matrix, because if there are a large number of people in the testing department and each person writes some tests, there will be a great deal of clustering around major functions.

This creates redundancy or overlap. It also results in many functions not being tested, or gaps. In the corporate environment, it is very important to achieve the maximum results for the minimum number of tests so it is best to ensure test cases cover all functions and there is as little overlap as possible.

Test Early in the Game

For each phase of the development, there should be tests and a testing lifecycle. The software testing lifecycle should correspond with the development lifecycle. Planning for testing should begin at the same time as the development begins its development planning.

This makes the test team more prepared to test. It also enables the use of standards across the testing and AD projects. If every single application is developed and tested in the same way, it makes work faster and easier.

Most corporations leave in-depth testing to the QA team (which gets involved after the code has been written) but some are now advocating that the programmers should also get involved in the testing and QA process. It is easier and less expensive to test early, and testing while code is being written offers many advantages in terms of time and effort saved.

If a programmer finds a bug while writing code, it can be repaired immediately. If the application goes to the QA team and comes back eight months later, the programmer may have forgotten what had been written. Worse still, the programmer may have left the company.

Getting Tools for Programmers

Programmers, like QA and test teams, are interested in quality. However, there are certain things they seek in their tools. They must be easy to use, non-intrusive to the programming cycle so programmers do not get distracted, and there must be an immediate impact on code quality.

Using a complex methodology that will give results in three months' time is useless for programmers because they are judged on a week-to-week basis.

What to Look for in Testing Tools

There are several things to consider when selecting a testing tool:

- *Learning Curve.* How easy will the tool be to learn and to use? Will it be easy to return to after some time has lapsed?

- *Test Suite Creation.* How much work must be put into create the test suites? Will the test suites be easy to understand? How easy?

- *Maintenance.* How easy will it be to change the tests to reflect changes in the target software throughout all stages of the software lifecycle?

- *Resilience.* Can the tool build tests independent of GUI changes? Does it handle non-standard Microsoft Windows facilities?

- *Error Recovery.* Does the tool have powerful recovery abilities? Can it ensure the scripts run reliably?

- *Test Management.* What facilities does the tool provide to manage the large number of scripts provided?

- *Independence.* The tool should not be confined to testing at the bitmap level; it must be able to record in a position- and size-independent manner. The tool must be able to recognize and test individual components of a window, check text, and compare response timing and DOS files.

Automation

As applications become increasingly complicated, testing them takes longer and becomes more mundane. Increasingly, vendors are offering automated testing tools.

Why Automate Testing?

Automated testing tools can repeat tests endlessly, faster than people can. They can be scheduled to conduct tests during off-peak hours and can simulate conditions people cannot. For example, one form of stress testing requires several people to hit the "Execute" button at the same time, to see how big a workload an application can handle. An automated system can ensure that all the "Execute" orders are synchronized, to a far higher degree than people can.

One CASE tools vendor was receiving reports from end-users of a mysterious bug its developers and QA personnel were unable to pinpoint. Manual testers, in the course of their normal 10-hour day, were not able to replicate the problem causing the product to freeze. By automating its test plan, the vendor was able to repeat the test cycle thousands of times over a 72-hour period.

Through taking repeated snapshots of memory throughout the testing process, developers were able to detect memory leakage. Manual testing could never have enabled the firm to locate and solve the problem.

The need to automate testing is great – about 25% of the average application is rewritten over the course of a year. Also, operating systems are constantly upgraded and corporations are always acquiring new utilities.

Automating the testing process enables a firm to keep costs down while increasing the frequency and number of tests being run – skilled manpower is expensive. Automation also provides corporations a repository of information which can be kept in a test library so it is not affected by personnel changes. Further, automation can help establish workflow scenarios that replicate real-world scenarios.

The Trouble with Automation

Before going off to automate its testing processes, a corporation must ensure it has defined the tests it wants to automate. Automation takes time, requires a commitment and investment in time, money, and people to be effective.

Definition and planning are very important because automated test suites will run over a long period of time. Corporations must plan what they want to test, how they are going to validate the results, how they are going to automate their tests, and how they will ensure the automation is working correctly.

Testing Tools

The following section provides brief descriptions of many of the testing tools currently on the market.

ATF – the Softbridge Automated Test Facility, from Softbridge, Inc., Cambridge, Massachusetts. Tel. 617-576-2257.

ATF is a complete software system designed to automate unattended regression testing of standalone or C/S applications. It is a software-only testing solution and requires no additional or special hardware. It is currently available for Microsoft Windows 3.0 and higher, OS/2 1.3, 2.0, and 2.1, and for Microsoft Windows NT.

ATF completely automates regression testing in the C/S environment, allowing users to run tests during off-peak periods when demand for computing resources are low. ATF's architecture enables true, unattended, automated testing – the software's intelligence is concentrated in one central point from which tests are executed. This architecture also enables users to repeatedly drive a distributed application as if it were a logical whole, while allowing complete autonomy at the individual test workstation.

Figure 7.1 Automated Test Facility Software Components

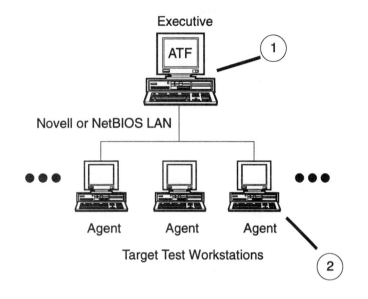

Executive

ATF

1

Novell or NetBIOS LAN

Agent   Agent   Agent

Target Test Workstations

2

ATF is comprised of two software components: 1) the Executive, and
2) the Agent.

Source: Softbridge, Inc.

ATF is divided into Executive and Agent packages. The Executive is an OS/2 application which provides a command center from which up to 50 target test workstations can be controlled simultaneously across a NetBIOS or internetwork packet exchange (IPX) LAN. Test cases are codified or "scripted" at the Executive, and implemented on target test workstations equipped with ATFs Agent software. This is illustrated in Figure 7.1.

The Agent software resides on the target test workstation. It can run tests on Microsoft Windows and OS/2 applications. The agent acts as an intermediary between the Executive and the application being tested. The Agent includes a powerful capture/playback facility. It captures a user's interaction with the application being tested – keystrokes and mouse movements. The interaction is stored in a fully editable file.

ATFs Executive is external to the applications under test. This enables ATF to recover from application, testing, and system errors. ATF can branch

---

conditionally, based on window status, bitmap text, and data comparisons. It can also take recovery actions, ranging from sending an "okay" key to a screen, to powering down and rebooting a system – provided a serial power control interface and relay switch have been installed. This is illustrated in Figure 7.2.

In addition to regression testing, ATF is also used for high throughput testing of standalone applications, server load and concurrency testing, stress and limit testing, performance testing, compatibility testing, and integration testing.

Figure 7.2 Automated Test Facility Executive

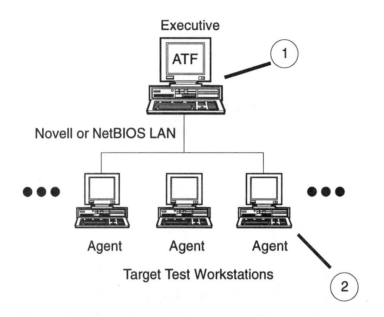

ATF is comprised of two software components: 1) the Executive, and 2) the Agent.

Source: Softbridge, Inc.

AutoTester for OS/2-PM and AutoTester 2.0 for Windows – *from AutoTester, Inc., Dallas, Texas. Tel. 214-368-1196.*

A testing tool for OS/2 Presentation Manager, AutoTester for OS/2-PM allows users to test graphical applications within OS/2. It uses an object-oriented, event-driven test automation process, rather than the clumsy bitmap method.

AutoTester 2.0 for Microsoft Windows is an advanced testing and verification tool for testing GUI applications. Its features include test synchronization, dynamic window placement and positioning, advanced control querying and manipulation, and actual text retrieval (regardless of text font or size).

Both AutoTester applications provide word processing-type editing of tests, including features such as cut/copy/paste, find/replace, and adjustable fonts. A toolbar is provided for quick access.

Instead of recording standalone keystrokes or mouse events with no reference to what they invoke, AutoTester records meaningful events, such as menu options or list box selections.

Test data is maintained in text files separate from the script so one script can be used to process multiple sets of test data. Testing can be performed in a structured, modular fashion for simplified test development and maintenance. This is enabled by a menu-driven front end in AutoTester's command set.

Complete, context-sensitive online help is available for all commands and functions, and commands are window-aware so users can be sure they are where they should be in the application.

AutoTester allows users to automate all phases of testing such as unit, acceptance, regression, and stress testing without the need for in-depth technical or programming knowledge. Users can compare context, text, and bitmaps for fully-automated, real-time decision making and conditional branching.

Confusion over font styles and sizes is eliminated because AutoTester stores graphics data as text for input or comparison, regardless of font style or size. International language and OS/2 text window support allow users to test OS/2 text sessions running under OS/2 Presentation Manager (PM) even if they are using international keyboards.

AutoTester traps TrapD/general protection fault (GPF) errors and can automatically reboot the computer after a system error occurs. It can work with third-party emulators, allowing users to test C/S and other applications distributed across remote platforms.

Full test documentation and custom reporting capabilities are part of AutoTester. All documentation is written in simple English so documenting tests and preserving application testing knowledge is easy. AutoTester's custom and automatic reporting capabilities help create test logs, track errors, and identify discrepancies as required.

System requirements for AutoTester for OS/2-PM are IBM 80386 compatible or PS/2, and OS/2 PM version 1.3 or higher.

System requirements for AutoTester for Windows are IBM 80386 compatible or PS/2, Microsoft Windows 3.0 running Enhanced Mode or higher (recommended) or Standard Mode. Supports a variety of terminal emulators, including IRMA, RUMBA, and EXTRA.

Platforms supported include IBM PC AT, PS/2 or compatibles running MS-DOS or PC-DOS 2.0 or higher. AutoTester 2.0 also supports a variety of terminal emulation and communications protocols, including AT&T, Data General, DEC, Hewlett-Packard (HP), IBM, Tandem, Unisys, and Wang.

AutoTester Plus Script Station – *from AutoTester, Inc., Dallas, Texas. Tel. 214-368-1196.*

This is an easy-to-use, menu-driven workstation for defining applications and generating structured, automated test scripts. Users describe their application in terms of basic components such as screens, fields, and keys. Once this is done, the Script Station provides a complete prototype environment for creating executable test cases in advance of coding.

Using information from existing code, CASE tools or text files, the Script Station enables users to automatically build test scripts tailored to their environment, then test them for compliance. The Script Station includes a standard script library which provides a base of scripts that can be easily customized for users' applications.

Test scripts are separated from test data to enable scripts to be reused and support higher volumes of testing. The Script Station's structured testing methodology creates a modular, automated operator which can apply, evaluate, and report a virtually unlimited volume of test cases.

There is only one point of maintenance for application changes, because the Script Station links the application user interface with the test script library. Application changes occur at the specification level and related scripts are simply regenerated. Table 7.1 lists the Script Station specifications.

Table 7.1 Specifications for Script Station

AutoTester Script Station IBM PC AT, PS/2 or compatibles.
MS-DOS, PC-DOS 2.0 or higher.
Requires 270K of conventional memory, or 55K with LIM 4.0-compliant expanded memory manager.
Supports color graphics adapters (CGA), enhanced graphic adapter (EGA), video graphics array (VGA), Hercules resolutions, and MOD 2, 3, 4, and 5 text video modes.
Supports a wide range of terminal emulation and communications protocols, including IBM, DEC, HP, NCR, Tandem, Wang, Unisys, and Data General.

AutoTester Plus Test Station – *from AutoTester, Inc., Dallas, Texas. Tel. 214-368-1196.*

The Test Station is an application-specific, automated test environment that lets users easily create, execute, and document test cases and scenarios. When combined with the AutoTester Plus Script Station, it provides a turnkey platform for building, executing, and documenting test cases on new or existing software.

The Test Station has a simple, intuitive menu system that allows users to create test data in the context of the system being tested. This minimizes training and improves productivity. Test cases can be created or modified to turn one case into hundreds of cases in minutes because simple narratives are used.

Test documentation is created simultaneously as test data is being entered. This ensures accuracy and transferability of testing. Test execution and reporting is accomplished by pressing one key.

The Test Station provides a complete prototype environment for creating executable tests before the application code is complete. Users can run a single test or a package of tests unattended, against their application, as many times as needed. Table 7.2 lists the Test Station specifications.

Table 7.2 Specifications for Test Station

AutoTester Test Station IBM PC AT, PS/2 or compatibles.
MS-DOS, PC-DOS 2.0 or higher.
Requires 270K of conventional memory or 55K with LIM 4.0-compliant expanded memory manager.
Supports CGA, EGA, VGA, Hercules resolutions, and MOD 2, 3, 4, and 5 text video modes.
Supports a wide range of terminal emulation and communications protocols, including IBM, DEC, HP, NCR, Tandem, Wang, Unisys, and Data General.

TestCenter 2.0 *– from CenterLine Software, Inc., Cambridge, Massachusetts. Tel. 617-498-3000.*

TestCenter claims to be the first software testing tool designed to help UNIX C and C++ programmers locate and correct program errors, while providing them with test coverage information to understand the thoroughness of their error checking and testing. (CenterLine is the developer of the ObjectCenter and CodeCenter UNIX C++ and C programming environments.)

TestCenter offers features for automatic runtime error checking and memory leak detection on executables. These are designed to enhance code quality and optimize program memory use.

It also offers graphical text coverage to help programmers more fully understand what portions of their application have and have not been tested for runtime errors, memory leaks or other customer-defined tests. In addition, TestCenter includes an intuitive GUI and querying facility to access test result files for enhanced productivity during test analysis and error correction.

New features added to version 2.0 include an error simulator, function-level code coverage, user-defined error checking, and support for threaded applications.

The error simulator lets programmers imitate a failure and simulate other conditions which could affect the behavior of the application, such as "out of memory" or "disk full" errors. The simulations are conducted during runtime. The simulator can be customized to simulate events specific to a user's application.

Function-level code coverage provides a higher-level view of where additional testing is needed. A new graphical cross-reference browser enables programmers to analyze which calls made in and out of a function were actually executed.

User-defined error checking allows programmers to insert application-specific and customized error checks into their applications. This is particularly useful for testing code when its source is not available, such as code obtained from libraries. The user-defined error checking feature is tightly integrated with TestCenter's GUI, so users can quickly visualize the results of their customized error checks.

Support for threaded applications is another new feature – TestCenter 2.0 supports testing applications which use Sun Microsystems, Inc.'s standard thread package for Solaris 2.x. TestCenter is available on Sun Microsystems, Inc. SPARC workstations running Solaris 1.0 (SunOS) and Solaris 2.3, and HP 9000 Series 700 and 800 workstations.

Sentinel – *from AIB Software Corp., Dulles, Virginia. Tel. 703-430-9247. AIB has acquired Virtual Technologies, Inc., the creator of Sentinel.*

Sentinel is a runtime memory access debugger for UNIX C and C++ programs, which provides runtime verification of pointer usage and dynamic memory allocation. It consists of a library of routines that can be linked into UNIX C and C++ programs to help programmers locate and resolve hidden bugs in the use of dynamic memory. Sentinel provides runtime verification of pointer usage and dynamic memory allocation.

It traps memory errors, traces stacks, and reports the source file, function name, and line number of the bugs. Sentinel also provides developers with the same level of information concerning memory allocation and, if applicable, where memory was freed or overwritten.

Sentinel claims to be the only memory debugging environment which runs on every UNIX platform. HP's SoftBench full-scale C and C++ development environment fully integrates a version of Sentinel.

Sentinel 2.0 will support HP's SoftBench on computers from HP and Sun Microsystems, Inc. It will also support IBM's implementation of SoftBench on the RS/6000.

The Sentinel debugging environment is supported on the following platforms: Solaris 2.1 on Intel 80386 platforms; Solaris 1.x (Sun OS 4.1.x) and Solaris 2.x on Sun Sparc-IIs and compatibles; HP-UX 8.xx and 9.xx on HP 9000/8xx/7xx systems; AIX 3.2 on the IBM RS/6000; UNIX System V Release 3.2 and 4.0 on Intel 80386 and 80486 systems; DG UX on Data General AViiON systems; IRIX on computers from Silicon Graphics, Inc.; Ultrix on DECstations from DEC; and Alpha OSF/1.

***DDTS** – from QualTrak Corp. Santa Clara, California. Tel. 408-748-9500.*

Hailed as the first commercial UNIX bug tracking system, Distributed Defect Tracking System (DDTS) conforms to standards of the Institute of Electrical and Electronic Engineers (IEEE), the U.S. Department of Defense (DOD), the International Standards Organization (ISO), and the Software Engineering Institute (SEI). DDTS is said to include the best features of in-house bug tracking systems developed by DEC, AT&T, Sun Microsystems, Inc., and HP.

DDTS works on both LANs and remote networks (Internet and UNIX-to-UNIX Copy [UUCP]). On LANs, it uses Network File System (NFS), Ethernet C/S user diagram protocol (UDP), and transmission control protocol (TCP) protocols. E-mail is used to scan for bugs in remote networks and QualTrak guarantees that no bug will ever be lost through the E-mail system. Both GUI and Tele Typewriter (TTY) are supported. DDTS has a defect organizer which keeps defects organized and separated into projects.

Features include a distributed database, a subscription feature which provides easy local access to defect information about remote projects, integration with source code revision control systems, flexible defect data fields; more than 20 types of management reports, and both a users manual and an online help system.

DDTS comes with more than 20 types of management reports, including:

- Defect arrival rate graphs

- Defect resolution rate graphs

- Bug counts by project and severity

- Bug counts by engineer and severity

- Bug counts by project and status

- Bug counts by engineer and status

- Full-page bug details

- Three-line bug summaries

- Summaries sorted by requested fields

QCAP – *from QualTrak Corp., Santa Clara, California. Tel. 408-748-9500*

QCAP is an X-11 GUI testing product. It tests multiple GUI applications on the same workstation simultaneously with no changes to the X-11 server or link-edited X libraries, so it does not need a dedicated workstation for testing.

QCAP is integrated with DDTS and allows contextual information about the test failure to be integrated directly into the defect tracker. QCAP uses a scripting language based on The Command Language (TCL), which is becoming a de facto industry standard for scripting languages in the UNIX market. It is shipped with a book on TCL.

Guido – *from QualTrak Corp., Santa Clara, California. Tel. 408-748-9500.*

Guido is a personal GUI tester for the developer. The first user interface-level debugger, it attaches a programmatic debugger to the GUI application being driven by a QCAP/Guido script, so the application is being simultaneously driven by the QCAP playback module and being examined by a programmatic debugger. If the application core dumps or fails, even after weeks of use, it can be replayed to reproduce the error. Guido produces QCAP scripts automatically, in effect creating tests automatically.

Automator QA *– from Direct Technology Ltd., New York, New York. Tel. 212-475-2747.*

Automator QA is an automatic operator or software robot equipped with an advanced and comprehensive QA testing ability. It develops tests and contains recovery routines if the target software performs unpredictably.

Automator QA combines an intelligent scripting language with four testing methodologies. Because it is an automated software testing tool, users can run unattended tests and conduct these tests during off-peak times.

Tests can be run as often as required. A detailed test log is maintained. Automator QA performs the functions of a human operator inputting data, logging responses, comparing actual with expected results, and logging a pass or fail. It will test any character-based application written in any language, running on any platform.

Automator QA is compatible with PC-DOS and MS-DOS. It can be used at all stages of software testing: unit, integration, system, stress, and acceptance testing. It can conduct regression testing, performance tests, response tests, and can be used to establish initial data files and set parameters for the test environment.

For large and/or complex systems, Automator QA with Navigator is recommended. Navigator builds a map of the entire system and carries out test programs according to the user's requirements.

All test activity is written to a log file. Information logged includes all keystrokes, route information (including failures), and passed and failed checks, together with actual and expected results.

If the software being tested performs unexpectedly, Navigator will use artificial intelligence techniques and automatically follow a series of error recovery strategies. Using these strategies will ensure the maximum number of chosen tests will be executed in an unattended run, increasing the effectiveness of the overall test run. Automator QA with Navigator is MS-DOS and PC-DOS compatible, and will test any character-based application written in any language running on any platform.

Automator QA with Navigator – *from Direct Technology Ltd., New York, New York. Tel. 212-475-2747.*

The same basic software testing tool as Automator QA (see above), but equipped with the Navigator module, designed to test large and/or complex systems. It builds a map of the entire system, from which it automatically carries out test programs.

Each application has three components: a map, tests, and a database of expected results. Each of these elements can be maintained separately. If the software tested behaves unexpectedly, Navigator uses artificial intelligence techniques and automatically follows a series of error recovery strategies. These strategies ensure the maximum number of chosen tests will be executed in an unattended run.

Navigator is compatible with PC-DOS and MS-DOS. It will test any character-based application, written in any language, running on any platform.

Vantive Quality – *from The Vantive Corp. (formerly known as ProActive, Software, Inc.), Mountain View, California. Tel. 415-691-1500.*

Vantive Quality is a QA management system that helps organizations comply with the ISO 9000 international quality standards. It covers the entire product lifecycle: design, development, production, installation, and maintenance.

Vantive Quality enables users to comply with goals defined in the ISO standards, including monitoring development phases, defining and monitoring quality objectives, managing product configurations, controlling changes and defects, validating product operations, tracking installations, maintaining specifications and documentation, supporting customers, and tracking problem resolutions and product releases.

There is a single repository of solutions to product problems in Vantive Quality. This repository can be accessed by the support, engineering, QA, sales, and marketing groups of a corporation.

Features of Vantive Quality include automatic problem escalation and dispatching, automatic communication of workarounds and fixes to the appropriate parties, support for standard classification of defects as defined in the IEEE 1044 standard, transparent links to popular software source and revision control systems, the ability to link defects to the specific level of product or assembly affected, and metrics, packaged reports, and ad hoc query support for real-time quality management.

PowerHouse Architect *– from Cognos, Inc., Ontario, Canada. Sales, service, and marketing: Tel. 617-229-6600.*

PowerHouse Architect is an integrated maintenance and documentation tool which automates testing, cross-referencing, and generates application documentation.

PowerRunner *– from Mercury Interactive Corp., Santa Clara, California. Tel. 408-987-0100.*

PowerRunner is an automated software quality system designed to improve the quality of C/S applications developed using Powersoft Corp.'s PowerBuilder. It can identify PowerBuilder custom objects, automatically verify the data behind DataWindows, verify drop-down objects, and use logical names assigned by PowerBuilder.

RAMexam *– from Qualitas, Inc., Bethesda, Maryland. Tel. 301-907-6700.*

Defective or damaged random access memory (RAM) is one of the most common causes of system crashes. Recently, many major hardware manufacturers are reported as using memory which does not use parity checking technology, making it even more important to use some sort of RAM checking tools.

Parity testing, however, catches only some errors some of the time, so a better testing system is required. Memory testing algorithms currently in use, including most power-on self-tests (which occur when a PC is turned on), are limited to reading and writing an arbitrary value into and from RAM.

RAMexam employs a consistent fault model based on the multiple known ways in which memory fails. This model employs a strategy of using specific sequences of bit patterns designed to detect specific types of memory failures – certain memory bits, for example, will fail only when specific other bits are changed to specific values.

RAMexam installs automatically and can be configured to test system memory at specified intervals – daily, weekly, monthly or as defined by the user. Various degrees of testing – from quick, short tests to exhaustive tests which may take all night to run – can be selected. Users can interact with RAMexam through its full screen interface or in a fully configurable batch mode. RAMexam works with MS-DOS memory management and recent releases of Quarterdeck Office System's QEMM and Helix Software's NetRoom.

LoadRunner – *Mercury Interactive Corp., Santa Clara, California. Tel. 408-987-0100.*

LoadRunner is an automated testing system for multiuser UNIX applications which can test C/S applications before they are deployed over a network.

It can emulate multiple users and distribute them over a network. A user can then control and monitor the C/S application from a single station. System performance can be tracked to a single transaction. Statistics are compiled graphically, so system performance can be easily analyzed.

LoadRunner is based on a virtual user technology which can test server behavior and client response time to balance, debug, and fine-tune a system. It works on workstations from Sun Microsystems, Inc. Support for HP boxes, Sun's Solaris environment, and a Microsoft Windows version are on the way.

BugBase for Windows/Network – *Archimedes Software, Inc., San Francisco, California. Tel. 415-567-4010.*

BugBase is a bug tracking tool which enables developers to define and track software defects and record, classify, assign, and report software bugs or change orders. It allows multiple users to access files simultaneously and has record locking and security features.

BugBase can create graphs which help developers detect trends based on software defects and stabilizations reported during a specified time. Pie charts can be used to break down the number of defects within a particular piece of software code.

Developers can save frequently-used filters to generate common reports, receive summary report lists of software defects including a brief account of each record and generate a detailed report listing all information about software defects of special interest.

SQA TeamTest for PowerBuilder 3.0 – *from Software Quality Automation, Inc., Woburn, Massachusetts. Tel. 617-932-0110.*

SQA TeamTest is a GUI testing tool for PowerSoft Corp.'s PowerBuilder development environment. It integrates automated test execution and repository-based workflow defect tracking.

Features include a configurable PowerBuilder object recognition model, expanded object state cases, customizable rules-based workflow, and a three-dimensional (3-D) graphics engine for the management and measurement of test results.

SQA TeamTest supports test planning, development, execution, results analysis, defect tracking, and summary reporting.

Chapter 8

CASE Tools

Overview

Computer-aided software tools (CASE) tools have traditionally been used only in the early stages of the software development lifecycle (SDLC). The SDLC consists of planning, analysis, design, construction, testing, production, and maintenance.

Increasingly, CASE is being used in all phases of software development and maintenance. Historically, there have been two major types of CASE: upper-CASE and lower-CASE. Each addresses different phases of the SDLC.

Upper-CASE

The most common form of CASE is upper-CASE. Also known as front-end CASE, it originated in computer-based design tools. Upper-CASE tools are used to help create clear and concise specifications for systems design. As such, they are used in the early stages of the software development lifecycle: problem analysis, systems analysis, flowcharting, and schematic design. They are typically PC-based or workstation-based, and many have direct links to workstations.

Lower-CASE

Also known as back-end CASE tools, lower-CASE tools are descended from applications generators, which are themselves descended from the first query-type 4GLs. These tools help in the coding stage of the SDLC. Designed to help automate software creation, they are used in testing, debugging, and maintenance.

In addition to creating lines of code, lower-CASE tools should provide automatic documentation, analysis capabilities for error checking and testing, and a data dictionary or central repository for creating and storing information about the system.

One advantage of lower-CASE tools is they allow developers to move systems development from the mainframe to the workstation or PC.

Integrated CASE

Upper-CASE and lower-CASE products have begun to merge to form integrated CASE (I-CASE). The idea is to build the application from end to end. However, the lack of standards for repositories has made it difficult to create I-CASE products because the repositories in different CASE products cannot communicate with each other.

CASE for Maintenance

Using CASE for the maintenance of existing programs, whether or not they were developed with CASE, is a recent phenomenon. It is also known as Computer-assisted Reengineering (CARE). CARE takes existing 3GL code, usually COBOL, and validates and recompiles it using CASE techniques, replacing spaghetti code with building blocks of modular and reusable code.

There are two types of processes associated with this. One is reengineering. Reengineering structures existing 3GL code into more modular and manageable 4GL code. The other process, reverse engineering, turns 3GL code into business rules, which can be manipulated with upper-CASE tools before being regenerated through lower-CASE.

Of the two, reverse engineering is the more difficult process. It can only be achieved after reengineering, and then only with a great deal of input from the analyst.

The Repository

Also called the encyclopedia, the term repository refers to a storehouse for all of an organization's business policies, strategies, and information on all its systems.

A repository contributes to improved consistency, increased productivity, and higher AD quality because it provides programmers with a consistent map of data and physical and logical dependencies. Thus, it acts as a single point of control which distributes information about programs and data to all relevant development and production applications.

Information stored in a repository should include information about all of an enterprise's methodology, data models, processes, and business rules. It should include details of the history of the project. This information is called metadata.

However, the repository should not contain information about the business itself; that is stored in traditional databases. For example, metadata may contain the definition of a sale and the rules relating to how a sale is processed; however, it will not contain the actual sales data.

The repository is typically based on an existing database. Increasingly, repositories are replacing data dictionaries. A data dictionary or library is a list of all data types used in a computer system. The repository does this one better: it cross-references all this information and adds meaning to it. Thus, a data dictionary contains raw information. The repository processes, cross-references, and analyzes this information.

All CASE systems use a repository or, at least, a data dictionary. The lack of standardization between repositories has been one of the factors limiting the ability of CASE tools to work with each other.

For large-scale development, a repository is essential. Consider the case of Prentice Hall Legal and Financial Services, based in New York City, for example. The firm had to convert proprietary applications running on Data General Corp. computers to UNIX running on a server from Sequent Computer Systems, Inc. It had not previously used a repository, and its developers did not formally share information.

Once the conversion project was launched, problems began to surface. Developers found reports that were not on any menu. Nobody knew what items were called. Different programmers knew different parts of applications. Different parts of an application were written in different languages.

Now, Prentice Hall is moving its development to Oracle Corp.'s CASE, which provides a central repository for analysis, design, and implementation definitions. Its new applications will revolve around complex customer billing.

In addition to containing information, an AD repository performs services to help manage the development and deployment process. These include version control through the use of check-in/check-out facilities, automatic capture of changes to information, facilities to import and export information to and from the repository, validity checking to enforce business rules, and impact analysis, security, and reporting.

Active versus Passive Repositories

A repository can be active or passive. Active repositories participate in the actual creation and running of the application by assembling the correct components at runtime and perform some precompiling. Passive repositories capture, maintain, and provide access to the metadata, but, after the design stage, they only do reporting and analysis. They are more like data dictionaries.

The trend today is toward active repositories. They are critical for C/S and object-oriented development. However, active repositories have their drawbacks – they can suffer from performance problems. Also, they are more difficult to implement. Many vendors are building repositories that can be used as either active or passive repositories.

Lack of Enterprisewide Repositories

While AD tool repositories are effective for use among members of a development team, they do not have the multitool support, flexibility and management, impact analysis, comprehensive management reporting, and integration with other tools to support enterprisewide modeling. This has led many organizations to deploy several repositories, each associated with different tools, and exchange and coordinate information between the various repositories and tools.

For example, GE Capital Mortgage Corp., of Raleigh, North Carolina, uses the repository that comes with Cadre's ObjectTeam set of development tools to store and manage the various design elements it creates with Cadre. However, its enterprise model resides in the IEF Encyclopedia from TI. Applications are also developed with IBM's Visual Age. Smalltalk stubs are generated with Cadre and imported into Visual Age. The company also incorporates IEF entities into Cadre designs.

Standards for Repositories

As stated earlier, repositories from different vendors cannot communicate with one another. Each vendor is developing its own API, and the number of APIs on the market is proliferating rapidly. There are two industry initiatives which may provide a long-term solution to this problem.

One is the development of the CASE Data Interchange Format. This provides a standard format for the structure and a format in which a tool presents its information.

The other is the portable common tools environment (PCTE). This promises to provide the full framework for an open system repository. The PCTE standard provides a public schema mechanism which lets independently-sourced tools access and manipulate common information in the repository.

Whether these initiatives are accepted throughout the industry remains to be seen. Microsoft Corp. and TI have already announced that they will jointly develop an open, scalable, C/S repository. They said the technology would be object-based and highly layered so pieces of it can be quickly changed. Storage of the data will be split from the view of the data so an underlying engine can support multiple views. The first versions will run on Microsoft Windows NT, but will support platform-independent modeling and generate applications for multiple platforms.

It must be noted that, while the two have promised an open process, they have not indicated that they will go to a standards body such as the American National Standards Institute (ANSI); they will only solicit input from independent software vendors, and do what they think best. With Microsoft behind the effort, many feel it could be viable. That will mean Microsoft and TI will have a monopoly of the market.

The Marriage of CASE and ADT

Linking applications development tools with CASE packages allows the tools to support more complicated applications. While applications development tools build GUIs, compile and debug code, and help provide links to database management systems, CASE tools examine and interpret programming code to ensure programming logic flows smoothly and programming sequences are correct.

Partnerships between the two are a logical step, and many AD tool vendors are looking to join CASE vendors. As discussed in the previous section, TI has teamed with Microsoft Corp. to develop a repository which would allow software developers to store common information more easily. TI is also porting its CASE tools to Microsoft's Windows NT OS.

Meanwhile, Learmoth & Burchett Managed Systems (LBMS), Inc., a Houston, Texas-based PC CASE tool developer, has developed a link from its System Engineer (SE) CASE design tool to Powersoft's PowerBuilder 3.0. This allows users to manage objects regardless of where they were created so they can reuse common objects and data models. LBMS has also teamed with Microsoft, announcing SE/Open for Visual Basic.

Bachman Information Systems, of Burlington, Massachusetts, has linked its Database Designer tool to PowerBuilder. Bachman Generator for PowerBuilder moves Bachman data models into PowerBuilder.

Gupta Technologies, Inc., based in Menlo Park, California, has announced its own CASE program, Tools Integration for the Enterprise (TIE). Uniface Corp., of Alameda, California, has unveiled Uniface Model Synchronizer, with which it is building links from its applications development language repository to 16 CASE tool repositories.

CASE Tools Vendors

EasyCASE Professional 4.0 – from Evergreen CASE Tools, Inc., Redmond, Washington. Tel. 206-881-5149.

EasyCASE Professional 4.0 is a CASE tool for the PC. It supports a variety of available structured methodologies for event, process or information modeling. It includes an integrated data dictionary, an online methodology monitor for analysis and checking, and a chart editor. This product is available for MS-DOS and Microsoft Windows. EasyCASE Professional 4.0 has links to PowerBuilder and SQL Windows.

EasyCASE Systems Designer – *from Evergreen CASE Tools, Redmond, Washington. Tel. 206-881-5149.*

Another CASE tool for the PC, EasyCASE Systems Designer has all the features of EasyCASE Professional. In addition, it has an automatic database scheme generation system for X/Base and SQL. It is available for MS-DOS and Microsoft Windows.

Bachman/Analyst – *from Bachman Information Systems, Inc., Burlington, Massachusetts. Tel. 617-273-9003.*

Bachman/Analyst is a fully integrated product for reengineering and building data models from legacy data structures. It runs on Microsoft Windows and OS/2 and has an open architecture. The product offers links to PowerBuilder, Synon/2E, and Intersolv/APS.

ER-Modeler – *from Chen & Associates, Inc., Baton Rouge, Louisiana.*

ER-Modeler offers a data and process modeling schema generation and reverse engineering capabilities. It runs on Microsoft Windows, UNIX and AIX. It has links to PowerBuilder, KnowledgeWare/ObjectView, and SQLWindows.

SilverRun-ADE – *from Computer Systems Advisers, Inc., Woodcliff Lake, New Jersey. Tel. 201-391-6500.*

SilverRun-ADE offers data and object-oriented development. It has distributed application generators and an open architecture. The product bridges to Synon/2E, Uniface, Progress 7.x, and Omnis 7. It runs on Microsoft Windows, OS/2, and Apple Macintosh.

ERwin/ERX – *from Logic Works Inc., Princeton, New Jersey. Tel. 609-243-0088.*

ERwin/ERX lets users build C/S applications. It has diagramming tools and offers forward and reverse engineering in addition to Microsoft Windows GUI capability. The package runs under Microsoft Windows, UNIX, Apple Macintosh, and Sun/OS. It has links to PowerBuilder, SQLWindows, and Visual Basic.

Cradle SEE – *from Mesa Systems Guild, Inc., Providence, Rhode Island.*

Cradle SEE provides application analysis and design, simulation, forward and reverse engineering, and document generation. It runs under UNIX, VMS, Ultrix, AIX, HP/UX, and SunOS. The package has links to SQLWindows and PowerBuilder.

Oracle CASE – *from Oracle Corp., Redwood Shores, California. Tel. 415-506-7000.*

Oracle CASE is a repository product which offers integrated tools, design automation, dataflow diagrams, application generation, reverse engineering, reengineering, and 3GL options. It runs under Microsoft Windows, SunOS, OS/2, OpenVMS, and UNIX. The package has links to Oracle Forms.

Oracle CDE, Oracle Forms, PL/SQL, Oracle Graphics, Oracle Card, Oracle CASE, Oracle CASE – *from Oracle Corp., Redwood Shores, California. Tel. 415-506-7000.*

Oracle CDE is an environment which can be divided into three main areas of functionality: Oracle CASE, which deals with the specification, design and generation of applications; the AD tools (Oracle Card, Oracle Glue, Oracle Forms, Oracle Reports, and Oracle Graphics) which deal with application building; and end-user tools such as Oracle Data Browser, Oracle Data Query, and Oracle Book which enable the interrogation and reporting on data from a variety of sources with a minimum of skills requirements.

CDE includes totally re-engineered versions of SQLForms (now called Oracle Forms) and SQL*ReportWriter (now called Oracle Reports). Oracle Graphics, Data Browser, Data Query, Oracle Book and Oracle Glue are also new. Recent versions of the CASE tools have been developed to work under Microsoft Windows and support developers on PC platforms.

The Application Building tools in CDE are composed of three layers – the basic enabling technology (database management, procedural language [PL]/SQL language, and user interface management); the reusability layer (the repository, code reuse and a virtual graphics system); and the tools themselves (Forms, Reports, and Graphics). These building tools cater to the three layers of systems functionality: data, language, and presentation. This is illustrated in Figure 8.1.

Figure 8.1 Oracle Common Desktop Environment Architecture

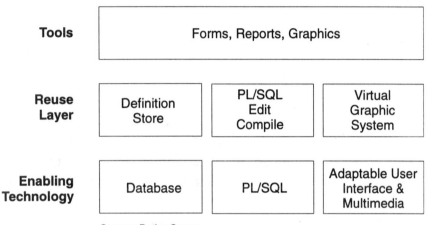

Source: Butler Group

The reuse layer is a particularly powerful feature of this architecture. It allows data definitions, PL/SQL code and presentation objects to be reused by the appropriate tools. The Oracle CASE tools act as a means of specification and generation of these entities and cater to issues such as version control.

Oracle Forms has an internal architecture which lets it participate in the common desktop environment (CDE) reusability layer. GUI support has been added, particularly for Microsoft Windows. Oracle Forms supports the creation and maintenance of forms-based applications with little or no coding for the more straightforward applications. Forms are created with a screen painter which supports cut and paste, multiple pages, graphics, background text, pop-up windows, and updateable scrolled areas.

Code is introduced to Oracle Forms applications through triggers. These triggers are event-driven and offer a highly structured mechanism for adding functionality to Oracle Forms applications.

Transparent support is provided for a variety of user interfaces, including Apple Macintosh, OSF/Motif, Open Look and Microsoft Windows. The tight integration of Forms with Reports and Graphics ensures Forms can use them easily to create highly functional forms-based applications.

One of the main problems with the early 4GLs was that they had a very high level of non-procedural functionality. This meant that the processing and display of forms could typically be controlled by statements which specified what was to be done, not how it was to be done. Oracle re-introduced a procedural element through PL/SQL.

PL/SQL can be implemented either within the tools or in the stored procedures and triggers provided by an Oracle 7 database within the procedural option. PL/SQL has a well-defined block structure which encourages structured programming.

Oracle Graphics supports the creation of business graphics such as bar and pie charts and a more general environment for the creation of graphical information. This includes integration with database data and other sources of line art and bit-mapped data. Charts can be linked and updated automatically.

More than 50 charts and more than 60 chart parameters are supported. Data for these charts can be retrieved using SQL statements against Oracle databases. Drawing tools including line, rectangle, ellipse, polygon, arc, and free-hand are also supported. These can be combined with charts.

Oracle Graphics can share data and displays with Forms and Reports. Using the "what you see is what you get" (WYSIWYG) graphical layout editor shared by the three, programmers can quickly build decision support solutions which can include sophisticated features such as multiple active windows and the ability to drill down from summary to detail.

Oracle Graphics allows users to define templates to reuse elements of displays. Its default charting capabilities reduce the need to write code manually. Once code is created, it can be reused across many systems.

Oracle Card can be used at any stage of the development lifecycle. It provides an easy method of prototyping, building, testing, and deploying graphical C/S applications. Oracle Card is fully portable, and runs in both Microsoft Windows and Apple Macintosh environments without manual conversion.

Oracle Card uses the HyperCard metaphor of cards, stacks, fields, and buttons. It automatically creates database fields, activates complex functions with simple buttons, and enforces master-detail relationships using a point-and-click interface.

Oracle sees CASE tools as effective utilities which accelerate the application building and maintenance process, but are not separate from it. It believes the only useful CASE is I-CASE.

Oracle CASE Designer supports the creation of Entity Relationship diagrams, Function Hierarchy Diagrams, DataFlow Diagrams, and Matrix Diagrams. Definitions are loaded directly into the data dictionary and are used as a basis for AD.

Oracle CASE Dictionary is a multiuser data dictionary which acts as a central repository for all the definitions that constitute an application. It is an active dictionary. Features include function decomposition analysis, dataflow modeling, module specification, data model analysis, and utilities for default database design, default application design, database sizing and reporting on dictionary objects and their relationships.

Oracle CASE Generators produce Oracle Forms, Oracle Reports, and SQL*Plus code. The definitions created through CASE Designer and held in the dictionary are used to generate applications.

One of the most powerful features in the generator products is preference control. This allows preferences such as form layout, coding style, and other application generation variables, to be specified once and reused with every generation.

Figure 8.2 Oracle CASE Architecture

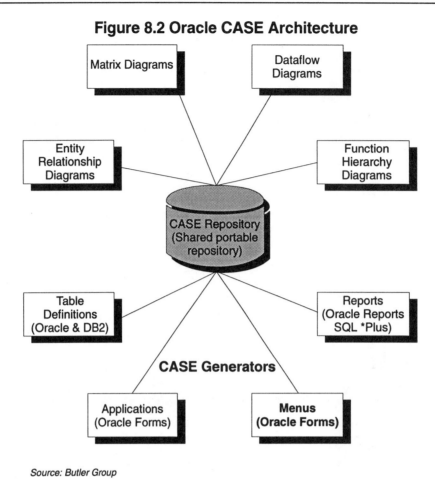

Source: Butler Group

Visible Analyst Workbench – *from Visible Systems Corp., Waltham, Massachusetts. Tel. 617-890-2273.*

Visible Analyst Workbench offers planning analysis, design, code generation, and reverse engineering for SQL and COBOL. It runs under Microsoft Windows and UNIX. The package has links to PowerBuilder, SQLWindows, and Uniface.

System Engineer 5.0 *– LBMS, Inc., Houston, Texas. Tel. 713-623-0414.*

LBMS has developed a link from its SE 5.0 CASE design tool to Powersoft's PowerBuilder 3.0 which users to manage objects regardless of where they were created and reuse common objects and data models.

Figure 8.3 Learmoth & Burchett Management Systems Smoothes Link to PowerBuilder

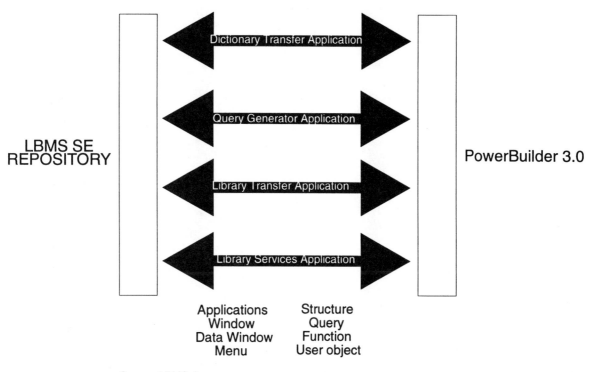

New link between LBMS and PowerSoft offers
bidirectional data exchange

LBMS SE
REPOSITORY

Dictionary Transfer Application

Query Generator Application

Library Transfer Application

Library Services Application

PowerBuilder 3.0

Applications   Structure
Window   Query
Data Window   Function
Menu   User object

Source: LBMS, Inc.

SE is said to be the first interface to support bidirectional exchange of data between PowerBuilder and another company's development tool through a central depository. GUI objects created in PowerBuilder 3.0 can be stored in SE 5.0's repository, where developers have access to version control, configuration management, and security. LBMS' SE/Stor and Powersoft's APIs are used to handle the bidirectional transfer of the objects, as illustrated in Figure 8.3.

Developers can open PowerBuilder, launch SE from an icon on the core panel in PowerBuilder, create the design for an application and then return to PowerBuilder. The results of the design will then be in PowerBuilder. By reading PowerBuilder applications, designers can also reverse-engineer graphical design models in SE.

First Data Corp., a credit-card firm located in Omaha, Nebraska, is looking to use the bidirectional support. Its AD team designed applications with LBMS and then created them with PowerBuilder. Exporting files from SE to PowerBuilder was an awkward process.

With the new links, exporting files from SE to PowerBuilder will be smoother, and the First Data Corp. development team will also be able to model inheritance of Microsoft Windows within PowerBuilder and manage security for its applications from within PowerBuilder. Separately, LBMS has teamed up with Microsoft, announcing SE/Open for Visual Basic.

Softbench Development Environment – *from Hewlett-Packard Co., Palo Alto, California. Tel. 415-857-1501.*

Softbench Development Environment enables development for heterogeneous systems. It offers integrated tools, visualization for new and existing code, and SQL support. The package runs under HP/UX, UNIX, AIX, and Solaris. It has links to Cadre/TeamWork, JAM, and Uniface.

IE:Advantage – *from Information Engineering Systems Corp., Alexandria, Virginia. Tel. 703-739-2242.*

IE:Advantage automates business planning, data and process modeling, and system design and implementation. It runs under Microsoft Windows 3.x. It has links to Synon/2E, PowerBuilder, and Intersolv/APS.

Excelerator II – *from Intersolv, Inc., Rockville, Maryland. Tel. 301-230-3200.*

Excelerator II offers analysis and design, software configuration management, modeling and document generation, and has a multiuser LAN repository. It also has a diagram editor. The package runs under Microsoft Windows, UNIX, and OS/2. It has links to PowerBuilder and SQL Windows.

System Architect – *Popkin Software & Systems, Inc., New York, New York. Tel. 212-571-3434.*

System Architect (SA) works with multiple methodologies – Yourdon/DeMarco, Gane & Sarson, Ward & Mellor, Shlaer/Mellor, Information Engineering, and SSADM.

SA works on IBM PCs and compatibles running Microsoft Windows or OS/2 PM. It comes with an integrated data dictionary which users can customize. Other features are automated documentation, extensible dictionary, normalization, rules, and balancing, requirements traceability, import/export; and custom reporting.

Several optional modules are offered. These include:

- *SA Reverse Data Engineer* provides reverse engineering of SQL databases, including DB2, Informix, Oracle, and SQL Server.

  Existing SQL databases can be brought into a CASE environment for management, enhancement, and/or forward engineering. SA Reverse Data Engineer provides for the generation of graphic screens and menus from .DGL and .MNU files. It also ensures new SQL databases are built with the proper design integrity.

- *SA Screen Painter* automatically creates screens for GUI or character-based applications from the SA Data Dictionary, captures existing screens, and provides a tool for designing screens from the beginning. Alternatively, all three methods can be mixed and matched.

  Screen Painter also generates Microsoft Windows dialogs and Microsoft Microfocus COBOL Screen Sections.

- *SA Schema Generator* translates entity models from the encyclopedia into schema for DB2, Oracle, Ingres, SQL Server, Rdb, Progress, Paradox, SQL Base, AS/400 (SQL & DDS), Interbase, OS/2 DBMS, dBase III, XDB, Sybase, and Informix. It generates Windows DLGs, and C-type data definitions or COBOL data structures.

- *SA Object-oriented Analysis and Design (OOA/OOD)* supports the Booch '91 and Coad/Yourdon methodologies.

- *SA Network Version* offers diagram and data dictionary record locking so multiple project members can work on the same project concurrently.

Information Engineering Facility for Client/Server – *from Texas Instruments. Inc., Dallas, Texas. Tel. 214-575-5729.*

IEF for C/S is a model-driven CASE tool kit which uses business specifications to model the complexity of C/S applications.

It supports multiple C/S application styles. Coding has been eliminated so users can select the optimum style for each application. This does away with the need to learn a new set of skills for each application. With the IEF for C/S toolset, a developer can model, build, and test an application before installing it into production.

When there are changes in business, developers make changes to the business specification. The code is automatically generated and can be tested in the IEF Developer Workstation before the application is installed in production.

The IEF toolset is an established AD suite which provides the controls and framework essential for C/S development. The IEF Developer Workstation is used to create and maintain business specification models. The IEF Encyclopedia, which is the backbone of model-level development, is the key to coordinating concurrent AD.

IEF for C/S supports multiple C/S application architectures, technologies, and platforms. Architectures include Distributed Process Implementation Tools for a MVS/DB2/CICS server, HP/UX, and AIX servers with the Oracle and Ingres databases, OS/2, and Microsoft Windows 3.1 clients. The C/S application architectures are supported by industry-standard PC LAN and WAN communication protocols.

Development tools include Developer Workstation for OS/2, Windows 3.1, HP/UX, Digital VMS, and the Encyclopedia for OS/2, HP/UX, and Digital VMS.

There is also the Graphical Application Facility (GrAF) family of products which is offered for use with IEF for C/S systems. GrAF lets users interact dynamically with application data through real-time views of current information in an interactive, dynamic way.

GrAF emphasizes complex visual representation styles typically required for operations control, scheduling, financial analysis, asset management, decision support, and other activities. Its visual analysis capabilities allow users to visualize situations when the complexity of the data will not conform to numerical analysis or traditional reporting techniques.

With the multiple graphical view styles in GrAF, end-users select the information views they prefer. They receive data associated with not only graphical objects such as GANTT charts, bar charts, and image labels, but also with attributes such as colors, sizes, and icons. Data can be updated through direct manipulation of graphical objects.

IEF offers AD for various styles of C/S computing, as listed:

- *Distributed Process Client/Server.* This style of C/S has the presentation logic and GUI on the client, and the business logic on the data server. Distributed process components bridge PC LANs to large WAN servers. It is well-suited to accommodate a large number of users and optimize application performance.

  The entire application including client, server, and all intercommunication is developed as a coordinated whole from within a single IEF model. The IEF product includes all communications components that overcome the technical differences existing between the client and server environments.

  Clients "speak" to an IEF-supplied communications infrastructure component which is based on industry-standard communications protocols. This component converts the PC LAN protocol to the WAN protocol and delivers the message to the corporate resource server. The server's logic component performs the required operation on the data component and then returns the result to the client.

- *Remote Data Client/Server.* This style of C/S computing gives users easy connection to departmental servers. The presentation and logic components are packaged to operate on the client and access the data component on the server. The IEF Development Workstation creates application components which access the communications supplied by the user corporation's database vendor. Because these IEF workstation toolsets are used with any C/S style, users have a common development.

  Users can design and construct remote database applications for a wide range of C/S environments. They can take an application designed for a combination of client and server platforms, with any IEF-supported DBMS, and re-target it to different hardware and software environments without changing the design.

- *Remote Presentation Client/Server.* Here, only the user interface resides on the client. Processing logic, data and OSF Motif-based presentation components operate in a central location on the server. X/Window devices provide access to application components through the network. Remote presentation architecture allows deployment to a central location, and makes for easy application maintenance. It gives users the benefits of both centralized system management control and a C/S application.

Chapter 9

4GL Products

Overview

Fourth-generation languages (4GL) have evolved to the point where they incorporate GUIs and C/S technology, offer rapid prototyping, and are being linked with other tools for C/S AD (see Figure 9.1). A list of AD tools and vendors follows.

4GL Tools

***Powerhouse 4GL** – from Cognos, Inc., Ottawa, Ontario, Canada. Tel. 617-229-6600.*

Powerhouse is the most widely used 4GL on midrange computers, according to Cognos. In a single computer instruction, it captures operations which may take dozens to hundreds of lines of code in traditional 3GLs such as COBOL and C.

The robustness of Powerhouse lets users code 95% to 100% of an application. Users can directly access the file management and OS resources rather than going through 3GL libraries.

Figure 9.1 4GL from the 1960s to the 1990s

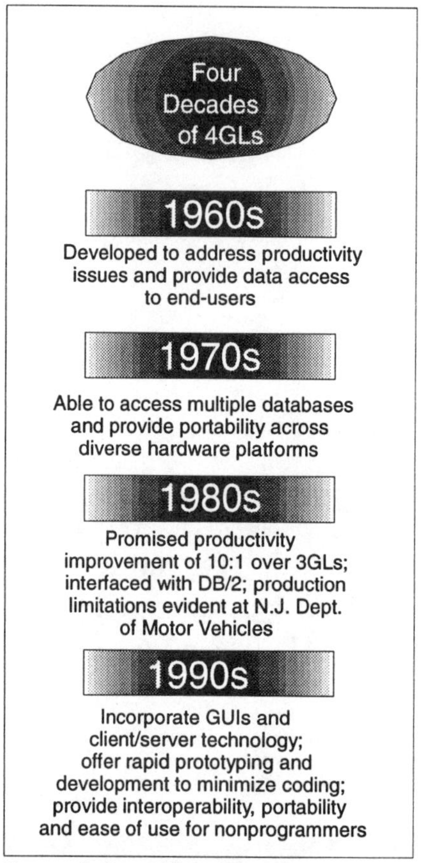

Source: Software Magazine

With Powerhouse, users build interactive, screen-based TP systems, volume processing applications, and complex reports. It is used in many *Fortune* 500 firms.

PowerDesigner – *from Cognos, Inc., Ottawa, Ontario, Canada. Tel. 617-229-6600.*

PowerDesigner is an analysis and design tool which uses a rules-based database to implement PowerDesign, the Cognos integrated set of graphical techniques for designing applications with the PowerHouse 4GL. This tool enables users to produce reports that detect and highlight all potential problems, inconsistencies, and omissions from the initial design stages.

Empress RDBMS and 4GL – *from Empress Software, Inc., Greenbelt, Maryland. Tel. 301-220-1919.*

Version 6.4 of Empress features Dynamic SQL which is compliant with the ANSI SQL 2 standard.

Dynamic SQL has been implemented as an extension of Empress' C precompiler. It includes features such as an RDBMS kernel which can be called from C, an application generator, and a full-function report writer.

Empress also offers multimedia data types and object-oriented capabilities. It produces high-performance applications which can be prototyped, developed, and executed in local or distributed mode.

Foxkit for Flagship – *from WorkGroup Solutions, Inc., Aurora, Colorado. Tel.: 303-699-7470.*

Foxkit for Flagship is a Microsoft Corp. FoxBase compatibility kit for the Flagship product from WorkGroup Solutions. Users can move FoxBase applications to Flagship, an Xbase 4GL database development system. It provides FoxBase programmers with access to various versions of UNIX supported by Flagship.

Nomad 3.4 – *from Must Software International, Norwalk, Connecticut. Tel. 203-845-5000.*

Nomad is an integrated set of 4GL information management tools designed for developing scalable applications using C/S technology. Users receive data management and reporting facilities, a windowed user interface, procedural language, nonprocedural 4GL, a developer's workbench, and a syntax-free reporting front-end.

Uniface Six – *from Uniface Corp., Alameda, California. Tel. 510-748-6145.*

Uniface's approach to AD tools is based on a rigorous modeling exercise. This forces developers to establish requirements at the conceptual level irrespective of the physical runtime environment.

The firm has announced Uniface Six, an integrated multiplatform 4GL development environment for creating flexible, scalable, and technology-independent applications. It comes with a set of tools to define, store, maintain the enterprise model. It also is able to rapidly generate and deploy applications which use an integrated model repository.

The Uniface Six development environment consists of six integrated workbenches which share information from an application objects repository. These are:

1. *Application Objects Repository* – for storing application models, data definitions, business rules, processing logic, global objects, and methods.

2. *Application Model Manager* – for creating and maintaining application models.

3. *Rapid Application Builder* – for the graphical creation of reports and forms.

4. *Deployment Manager* – which incorporates a system of native database drivers for transparent database access, application partitioning facilities, and distributed processing through interfaces to TP monitors and RPCs.

5. *Developer Services* – for managing team development with version control and access privileges facilities.

6. *Personal Series* – which end-users utilize to query data, build reports, and transfer data into popular desktop applications.

Figure 9.2 illustrates the Uniface Six model.

Development work begins with the Uniface Information Engineering and Design Facility. It follows a methodology which breaks the development process into three components: conceptual, external, and internal.

Figure 9.2 The Uniface Six
Model-driven Development

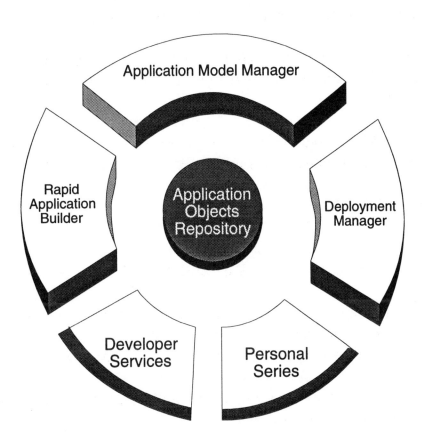

The conceptual schema is the central data dictionary, where developers identify field definitions and relationships with the modeling tools supplied. Developers also define data validation routines, computations, and business rules using either a 3GL or the Uniface 4GL.

The external schema allows external views of the information to be created. These include screens, reports, and other visual elements seen by the end-user. Instant Application Builder will help with the prototyping of screen elements.

In the internal schema, developers dictate how the data dictionary is physically managed. This includes where each database is located and how databases, reports, and screens are related. No coding is required to create connections across databases or perform updates on different databases simultaneously.

Uniface for OS/2 2.1 – *from Uniface Corp., Alameda, California. Tel. 510-748-6145.*

Uniface for OS/2 2.1 is a 4GL tool for developers who want to write C/S applications for the OS/2 platform. It provides a multiplatform environment including an integrated development environment, a forms-based application builder, a report writer, and a universal presentation interface for support of Microsoft Windows 3.1, Open Look, OSF/Motif, and the OS/2 Workplace Shell.

Uniface for OS/2 2.1 supports IBMs Multiple Document Interface so that applications have a consistent look and feel. It also supports IBMs Dynamic Data Exchange (DDE) and offers access to IBM DB2, DB2/2 and DB2/6000 DBMS. OS/2 objects are defined in the Uniface Model Repository for portability between Microsoft Windows, Open Look, and Motif.

The tool is platform-independent and DBMS-independent. It is available for MS-DOS, Microsoft Windows 3.1, VMS, HP MPE/ix, and most standard UNIX systems.

Brewers Retail, Inc., the sole distributor of beer in the Canadian province of Ontario, used Uniface to build a daily inventory measurement package when it decided to move business applications from an IBM mainframe to UNIX-based systems in 1990. It has since used Uniface to develop systems for ordering, time tracking, and operations control.

AD Workbench – *from KnowledgeWare, Inc., Atlanta, Georgia. Tel. 404-365-0246.*

KnowledgeWare has licensed R&O GmbH's Rochade repository and is offering it and two other tools – ADW/Workgroup Coordinator and ADW/Workgroup Manager – to target high-end C/S development.

The ADW/Workgroup Coordinator allows multiple developers to access ADW encyclopedias and synchronizes their work. When it is time to consolidate those separate encyclopedias, the ADW/Workgroup Manager is used.

The ADW/Workgroup Manager handles change management, security, and impact analysis. It consolidates the multiple encyclopedias into the Rochade repository. The Rochade repository will help control and manage multiple ADW encyclopedias and provide access to third-party tools.

Together, the three tools enable KnowledgeWare to manage the AD process at three levels (see Figure 9.3).

Figure 9.3 Client/Server Development Environment

KnowledgeWare's new tools target three development environments:

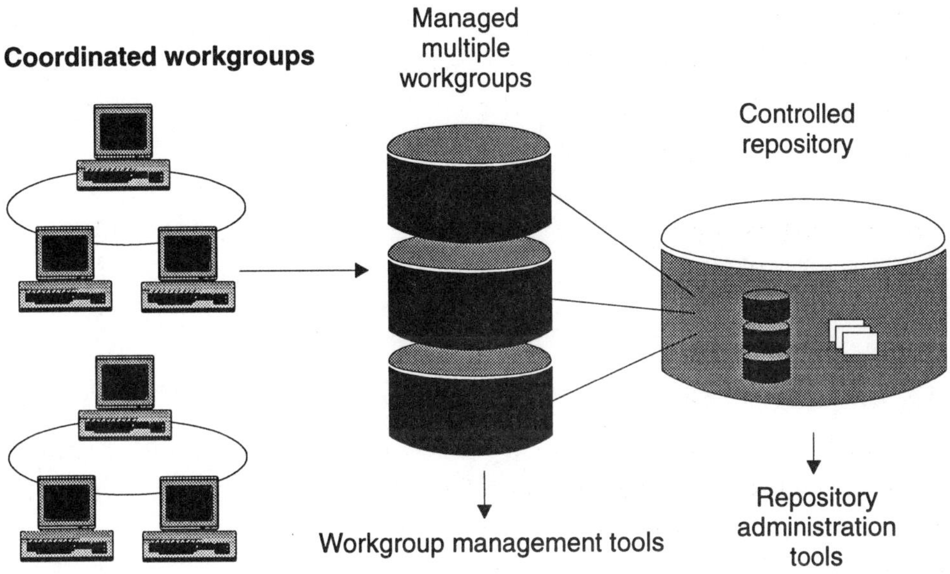

Source: Computerworld

KnowledgeWare ran into financial difficulties and was acquired by Sterling Software, Inc. in December 1994, which led to some uncertainty about the future of its tools. It is not yet clear how these will fit into Sterling's portfolio.

At least one KnowledgeWare customer has decided to switch AD platforms. First Union National Bank, based in Charlotte, North Carolina, has begun moving from ADW to Intersolv's Excelerator II tools because of KnowledgeWare's cumbersome and archaic product structure, inadequate support, and its financial difficulties.

NATURAL – from Software AG of North America, Inc., Reston, Virginia. Tel. 703-860-5050.

NATURAL combines a portable and executable specification language with a robust operational environment. It supports standard GUIs, including Microsoft Windows, OS/2 PM, and OSF/Motif.

Features include:

- Integrated source code and data definition editors;

- Screen/report painters with platform-standard GUI support, definable validation rules, and automatic handling of Help;

- Direct linkage with PREDICT, Software AG's integrated active data dictionary;

- Online testing and debugging facilities;

- Support for multiple DBMS engines, including ADABAS, DB2, Rdb, and IMS;

- An interactive optimizer compiler;

- Support for embedded ANSI-standard SQL with RDBMS-specific extensions; and

- Application portability without change, from mainframes to midrange machines such as HP 9000, Sun, IBM RS/6000, and SCO UNIX boxes to PCs.

The PREDICT active data dictionary documents and supports the management of all application information, including data components, process components, and the interactions between them. This model of users' applications is maintained dynamically: any modifications in PREDICT invoke automatic updates of all appropriate references.

NATURAL Engineering Workbench (NEW)/Define and NATURAL for Windows – from Software AG of North America, Inc., Reston, Virginia. Tel. 703-391-6769.

NEW/Define is a PC-based tool which supports the analysis phase of the application engineering lifecycle. NATURAL for Windows is a 4GL development environment which allows users to design, develop, prototype, test, deploy, manage, and maintain applications. Programs developed in NATURAL are source code-compatible across various operating systems. When used together, NEW/Define and NATURAL for Windows provide the capability to design and develop cross-platform applications.

NATURAL CONSTRUCT – *from Software AG of North America, Inc., Reston, Virginia. Tel. 703-860-5050.*

NATURAL CONSTRUCT is an application generation system which facilitates both rapid prototyping and the final development of complete business applications. It offers a quick and easy way to produce high-quality, environment-independent applications.

NATURAL CONSTRUCT uses a model concept for its generation process. It comes with a base of more than 65 predefined models. Developers can add to or modify this base, obtaining a set of pre-tested, fully-reusable models customized to the requirements of their corporation. NATURAL applications are generated from this base.

There are three interactive menu-driven subsystems in NATURAL CONSTRUCT:

1. *The Generation Subsystem* allows users to specify, generate, edit, test, and maintain a variety of NATURAL applications. It also allows automatic generation of the appropriate screen layouts. "Fill-in-the-blank" screens capture application specifications which are then fed into the user's customized models to generate optimized, fully functional business applications.

2. *The Help Text Subsystem* is an easy-to-use mechanism for creating and maintaining online help for all programs and fields in applications generated by NATURAL CONSTRUCT.

3. *The Administration Subsystem* is used to create new models and maintain existing models. This is the subsystem that allows users to customize

models to their organization's standards for code structure, documentation, security, and user interfaces.

Using NATURAL CONSTRUCT will give developers greater consistency in the look and feel of their applications. It will also increase their productivity.

Chapter 10

Object-oriented Programming

Overview

There are three main types of objects in object-oriented technology. The first is graphical objects, which are more often known as icons.

The second type consists of program objects or reusable software objects. These consist of groups of software modules – pre-set chunks of programming code – which can be linked on demand to create different applications, just as blocks used to create models. Using program objects saves money and programming and development time.

Reuse is at the core of all OOP plans. However, remember that reuse benefits will not be achieved until the second or third project. MIS staff at NationsBanc-CRT, the Chicago-based trading division of NationsBank Corp., took almost a year to determine how to reuse the objects stored in it's object library.

The third type of object is the managed object. This category can include computers, network devices, different types of LAN and WAN connections, databases, text files, data, and just about anything else.

This managed object approach is the one taken by Novadigm, Inc. of Mahwah, New Jersey in its electronic software distribution package, Enterprise Desktop Manager (EDM). EDM encapsulates information about a corporation's applications, files, hardware resources, software configurations, and the

---

installation methods required for applications into objects. Distribution of software across the enterprise is then a simple matter of dragging and dropping objects across the manager's workstation screen.

The term "object" is loosely used, so vendors should specify exactly what they mean when they claim their products are object-oriented or use OT.

Benefits of Object Technology

The advantage to using object development tools is that OOP enables developers to:

- create a better and closer representation of their business problem;
- re-use prototype code, develop complex functions more quickly; and
- perform simultaneous analysis and development.

Figure 10.1 illustrates the top benefits of moving to OT.

Figure 10.1 Top Business Benefits of Moving to Object Technology

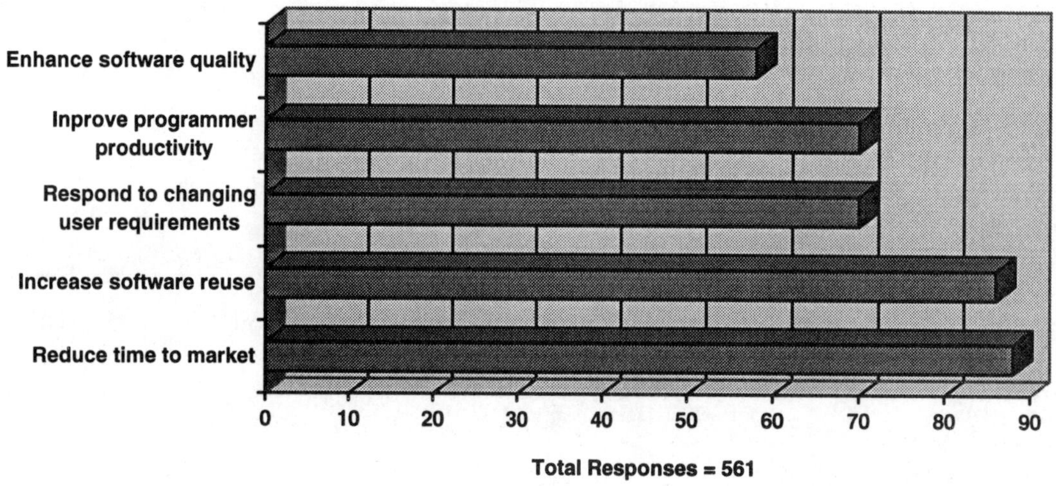

Total Responses = 561

Source: Market Perspectives, Inc.

Performing simultaneous analysis and development is the wave of the future. In fact, many believe building applications first is doing things backwards. Leilani Allen, the senior vice president of IT at PNC Mortgage Corp. of America, in Vernon Hills, Illinois, states IS should deal with the operations issues as it is doing AD because it simultaneously examines the network, the traffic, and how to build the C/S system.

BankAmerica Corp., the parent company of Bank of America, adopted this approach when building a distributed network management system using OT. The Bank of America has a data center in Concord, California which runs an SNA network connecting several IBM mainframes, 25,000 IBM PCs, and 1,500 OS/2 LANs at more than 1,000 sites across California. It needed a way of managing this SNA network configuration in addition to the configuration of complex, dynamic software on each network node.

The ideal solution should be distributed to minimize demands on each branch's limited bandwidth. It could use IBM's Systems Application Architecture (SAA) Advanced Peer-to-Peer Networking (APPN) protocol to provide program-to-program communications across the network. BankAmerica selected Digitalk, Inc.'s Smalltalk running on OS/2 as the implementation language.

Instead of hiring OT experts for its development team, BankAmerica selected people who could adapt quickly to change, had experience with more than one language, had a conceptual grasp of every aspect of the bank's network, and who were willing to work 12-hour days for the duration of the project.

The team did not use a formal methodology for analysis and design, but developed an iterative development methodology of its own. Development began in June 1991. By the end of that year, the team had the development infrastructure in place and had defined the problem domain. During the next six months, users were given increasingly refined development prototypes to test. This resulted in more than 600 changes to the user interface.

By September 1992, the development documentation had been created, and development of the production system began in October. By the end of November, the new Network Configuration Facility (NCF) was in place. Using the NCF, less than 12 operators were managing the configuration of the entire network.

The NCF architecture required an object persistency manager. This persistency manager was created using IBM DB2 and the OS/2 Database Manager. Several other management tools were also created by the team: object schema, relational schema, and object lifecycle management tools, all developed using Smalltalk. Unit-of-work management tools were developed using Smalltalk and CICS.

The reasons corporations are moving to OT are that it lets them develop applications faster, and the technology copies the way people work and communicate. Also, the methodology replaces the step- by-step programming techniques used in the C, COBOL, Fortran, and 4GL programming languages.

Drawbacks of Object Technology

The costs for training and tools are high, and BankAmerica found there was a six-month learning curve. Also, there is a shortage of tools suitable for team development, managing object lifecycles, testing and performance analysis, and the tools which are available come with inadequate documentation and example code.

For NationsBanc-CRT, which had a distributed network in place and built an object system from scratch, costs, including training, ranged from $2,500 to $8,000 per programmer in the first year alone. The total cost was 50% higher than if the bank had continued developing in C. The plus side is that the results justify these expenditures – after 18 months, NationsBanc-CRT was close to breaking even, and, after two years, it has achieved functionality which would not have been possible otherwise.

Employee training can take up 5% of the total operating cost of a C/S environment over a five-year period, according to studies from market research firm, The Gartner Group, Inc., of Stamford, Connecticut. This is second only to the 9% spent on hardware and software.

The best estimate is for companies to budget for half of a year's salary to train each IS staffer, according to market research firm Forrester Research, of Cambridge, Massachusetts. This includes the time lost while the employee is attending courses, and out-of-pocket expenses. Typically, these employees need instruction in relational databases, database access tools, C/S AD tools, and integration.

Compared to the cost of training central IS staff, training C/S staff is a pittance. According to Forrester Research, training an IS professional can cost $30,000 to $50,000 per person initially, and another $5,000 to $10,000 a year afterwards. See Table 10.1.

Table 10.1 The Five Percent Solution

		Small setup	Midsize setup	Large setup
End-user education	Number of end-users	20	200	5,000
	Cost per student per day	$150	$150	$150
	Year 1 training days	5 days	5 days	5 days
	Year 1 cost	$15,000	$150,000	$3.75M
	Years 2-5 training days	1 day	1 day	2 days
	Years 2-5 cost	$3,000	$30,000	$1.5M
End-user support staff training	Number of end-users	1	5	83
	Cost per student per day	$365	$365	$365
	Year 1 training days	20 days	18 days	18.1 days
	Year 1 cost	$7,300	$32,850	$549,325
	Years 2-5 training days	5 days	5 days	6 days
	Years 2-5 cost	$1,825	$9,125	$151,475
Application Development support staff education	Number of end-users	None	10	65
	Cost per student per day	N/A	$320	$320
	Year 1 training days	N/A	27.2 days	27.2 days
	Year 1 cost	N/A	$87,040	$478,720
	Years 2-5 training days	N/A	100 days	550 days
	Years 2-5 cost	N/A	$32,000	$176,000

Retraining Business Organizations for Object-oriented Programming

Learning OT and Smalltalk is, typically, only a fraction of the total training needed by the staff of a corporation. In many cases, people are being exposed to numerous changes at multiple levels at the same time when retraining for OOP.

For example, COBOL programmers converting to Smalltalk must learn C/S architecture versus mainframe architecture, Windows-based and mouse-based GUIs versus a 3270 forms-based interface, object-oriented thinking versus procedural thinking, Smalltalk versus COBOL, automatic memory management versus explicit memory management, OOA/OOD versus structured analysis and design, and a highly interactive integrated development environment versus a batch-oriented compiled development environment.

This massive series of changes means that, even with a good training program, the average individual takes about six months to reach functional proficiency in OOA/OOD or OOP.

Here are some insights on training from T.W. Cook, of ParcPlace Systems, Inc., who trains people in object-oriented concepts.

- *Focus on doing.* Concentrating on intensive classroom training alone will lead to burnout. The best programs alternate classroom instruction with focused, hands-on practice with the aid of an experienced mentor.

- *Do not try to learn everything at once.* People with a COBOL background, for example, are more comfortable if learning object concepts is separated from learning specific languages and tools.

- *Do not expect everyone to successfully make the transition.*

- *Do not expect staff to become experienced programmers overnight.* It takes about six months after the training program before people can be productive.

- *Experience is important.* People who have good common sense about what kinds of approaches do and do not work in the real world can usually find a way to translate that know-how to objects.

- *Communicate.* Object-based development is very communication-intensive, and it is important to understand what other development team members are doing and how they are doing it.

- *Train "just in time (JIT)."* Do not bundle training for the entire organization unless everyone will begin using the new technology immediately. Much of what has been taught will be forgotten if it is not applied and reinforced quickly.

Corporations should also train their managers to at least understand basic concepts about objects – what objects are, how they are found, and the basic ideas behind OOP technology. This will help them understand the conceptual issues being faced by their MIS organizations.

The Object Standard Wars

Currently, there is a battle in the OOA/OOD standards arena. Microsoft, with its common object model (COM), is feuding with the Boulder, Colorado-based Object Management Group (OMG), which is the major standards body in the object-oriented technology field.

The OMG offers the common object request broker architecture (CORBA). This defines object request broker (ORB) implementations, services, and interfaces. An ORB sits between object services on one hand, and application objects and common facilities on the other. It is the mechanism that sends and receives messages between objects in the OMG's object management architecture (OMA) which defines the primary parts of object-oriented computing environments.

CORBA is the result of the joint submission of a Request for Proposal (RFP) to OMG by DEC, HP, HyperDesk Corp., NCR Corp., Object Design, Inc., and SunSoft, Inc. They developed and supported a common platform featuring rapid commercial availability taking advantage of the previously developed technologies of each firm. Almost all major systems vendors, including IBM, Sun Microsystems, Inc., and HP, support CORBA.

Object Linking and Embedding (OLE) is Microsoft's technology for managing compound documents and objects on Microsoft Windows. Currently, OLE 2.0 allows desktop applications to be launched from within other applications. It also provides a common interface that allows applications to be assembled from preexisting software building blocks, called OLE controls.

For a while, it looked as if Microsoft and OMG would move in different directions which would force programmers to implement a variety of object models on an array of platforms.

At an OMG meeting in Dublin, Ireland in early September 1994, Microsoft stood behind an emerging specification which would allow its COM to interoperate with CORBA. Recently, Microsoft and DEC released a common COM specification for creating multiplatform OLE applications. Contrary to industry expectations, however, the COM does not include guidelines for interoperability between OLE and CORBA. This means that there is still no clear-cut standard for interoperating between these two major object models.

In early 1996, however, Microsoft will provide specifications to allow the CORBA model to interoperate with the COM, which will be ported to the UNIX platform to create links to Microsoft's OLE applications.

Using Object Technology to Interface with Legacy Applications

Typically, implementing applications using Smalltalk and C++ requires interfacing them to legacy systems. These interfaces take the form of an object-oriented representation of the relevant data and/or functionality of the legacy system.

The way the object-oriented application developer sees it, the legacy application is "wrapped" in an object-oriented interface. The wrapper code exists as part of the object-oriented application. The same wrapper code may be shared by multiple applications to the extent that they share an interest in the same entities, attributes, and functionality of the legacy system. Figure 10.2 illustrates the legacy system interface.

Many think the legacy system is always represented by a single object. This is only true when the legacy application is managing a single, complex object, such as a document or spreadsheet. In general, the legacy system manages a number of inter-related concepts, each of which must be represented as a wrapper object in the object-oriented environment.

Figure 10.2 Legacy System Interfaces

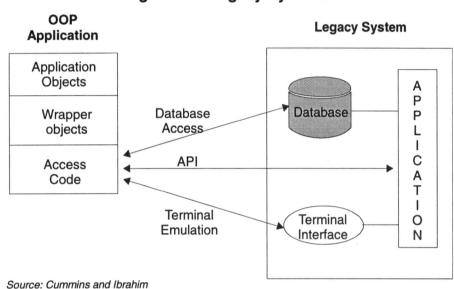

Source: Cummins and Ibrahim

Three Legacy Access Approaches

As shown in the figure, the legacy access code provides the interface to the legacy application. This code interfaces to the legacy system in one of three ways: direct database access, terminal emulation or API calls.

Direct database access is the most straightforward approach and should be restricted to applications not required to update the legacy database. If the application updates the legacy database, there is a strong risk the update will be incompatible with the legacy application.

The terminal emulation approach is most appropriate for an application that must update a legacy database. It enables the development of client applications which support interactive analysis and decision support. This approach also facilitates the integration of multiple legacy applications through a client-based, object-oriented application.

The API interface applies to legacy applications that operate in the workstation environment and provide a well-defined interface to legacy application functionality. These are primarily engineering applications where an object-oriented application, typically an artificial intelligence application, must interface to a vendor-supplied, computer-aided design (CAD) system.

Tips for Surviving Object-oriented Programming Projects

This section offers several tips for successful OOP projects.

- *Create a proper information model.* Without this, the project may run into trouble in the future.

  For example, a European country used an object-oriented system to replace a legacy system designed to track government benefits. The programmers identified object classes with generic names such as "pension" and "beneficiary." The system worked well, until it was time to update the legislative rules embedded throughout the program. Because a legislative rules object class had not been created, the programmers could not perform a global update. They had to change each legislative rule individually.

- *Ensure the development team has the right skill sets.* If it does not, find people with the necessary skills or send staff for training.

  It is preferable to train existing staff because they are already knowledgeable about the business. Training has another benefit: it makes staff more comfortable with the new technology. Often, resistance to change is based on unfamiliarity.

- *Look for help from people with experience.* There are many training programs and seminars run and attended by people with experience in OOP. Developers can network with them and get their advice. Developers can also turn to their local data processing association, their vendor, and join discussion groups on the Internet.

- *Start small.* Do not develop a full-scale pilot project – these take a long time, cost a great deal of money, and, if they fail, can lead the corporation to abandon the technology. Choose a project that will not put the corporation in trouble if it fails.

- *Keep the focus strictly on OOP.* Do not introduce other technologies at the same time OOP is implemented.

  There is too much to learn and there are too many things that can go wrong. If two new technologies must be introduced simultaneously, run concurrent pilot projects, and integrate them only after both are understood thoroughly.

- *Monitor the progress of the project.* This can be based on the number of compiler invocations per person, per module, and per unit of time, for example.

- *Stick to deadlines.* If the project delivery date slips, management will view the technology being promoted as a failure. If the deadline cannot be met, reduce, limit or restrict the scope of the features offered, but deliver the critical pieces on time.

Key Functions for Object-oriented Programming Application Development Tools

OOP AD tools should include:

- *A visual workbench.* This encompasses two groups: high-level, GUI-based visual development tools such as form painters, backed by rich, business-oriented classes and custom controls.

- *Repository management tools.* These are extensive data modeling and data definition facilities (metadata), repository-based application generation with bidirectional integration from database design through form generation up to code generation, and project and configuration management integrated with the repository.

- *Object and event technology.* This consists of full object- orientation and full support for the event-driven paradigm of modern user interfaces.

- *A compiler.* Efficient compiler technology, supporting 4GLs, COBOL, Xbase, and C is required, together with integrated analysis and debugging tools.

- *Database and connectivity services.* The requirements here are database independence with full support for advanced databases such as stored procedures, and application partitioning across heterogeneous platforms.

The Object Tools

CA-OpenROAD – from Computer Associates International, Inc., Islandia, New York. Tel. 516-342-5224.

CA-OpenROAD is a comprehensive, object-oriented, repository-driven AD tool suite based on CA-Windows 4GL from Ingres. It has a full suite of built-in development aids, including easy-to-use painters, a programming language, vendor-supplied class libraries, and debugging tools.

Because it is built around a full-function repository which coordinates data definitions and program elements, CA-OpenROAD can be used to generate complete object-oriented applications with a minimum of effort and a maximum of maintainability. CA-OpenROAD also incorporates CA-OpenROAD/Architect. This is a graphical CASE-like tool for data analysis and repository generation.

Repository-based form generation is simple: data is defined to the repository, either through a simple fill-in-the-blanks interface, or the even easier CA-OpenROAD/Architect graphical tool. Once the data is defined, forms are generated automatically with default graphical layouts and complete Create/Read/Update/Delete (CRUD) functionality.

These forms, in turn, generate CA-Windows 4GL code which can be modified as required. The modifications are preserved and applied automatically to the new default forms. Data definition changes propagate back to the CA-OpenROAD/Architect for complete bidirectional interoperability.

Repository-driven development also integrates seamlessly with the use of class libraries and custom controls which are themselves stored in the repository. CA-OpenROAD has a rich set of built-in class libraries. In addition, CA-OpenROAD can embed 3GL code as needed for maximum flexibility and performance. Finally, the repository provides inherent configuration management.

The object-oriented features of Ca-OpenROAD include unlimited encapsulation, unlimited user-defined classes, inheritance, and polymorphism.

Painting functionalities available let developers use CA-OpenROAD to build GUIs. CA-OpenROAD supports UNIX platforms and also offers a native Microsoft Windows look and feel. It will also offer native look and feel for future versions of Windows, such as Windows 95.

CA-OpenROAD is multithreaded and has an integrated stepper/debugger. In addition, it has powerful built-in query functionality. Its repository-driven architecture lets developers create complex database access logic using point-and-click commands.

Platforms supported are Microsoft Windows, Windows NT, OS/2 and UNIX/Motif. CA-OpenROAD supports all major RDMSs including CA-OpenIngres, Oracle, Microsoft SQL*Server, Sybase, Informix, CA-IDMS, CA-Datacom and DB2. It also supports several legacy non-relational DBMSs and file managers, such as IMS, VSAM and RMS.

CA-OpenROAD can generate stored procedures for various DBMSs, including CA-OpenIngres, Oracle, Sybase and Informix. This makes applications developed with CA-OpenROAD portable across most popular DBMSs. Further, the form generation capability includes Dynamic Data Links (DDLs) for a number of supported DBMSs.

PowerBuilder Enterprise Edition Version 3.0 – *from Powersoft Corp., Burlington, Massachusetts. Tel. 617-229-2200.*

Used together with PowerMaker Version 3.0, also from Powersoft, this product eases the transition from 3GLs to OOP. PowerBuilder offers a strong set of object-oriented features for developers, while PowerMaker captures the expertise of skilled developers and makes it available to less experienced developers and power users as form design templates.

PowerBuilder includes a complete, object-oriented form development environment, repository and database management, query, report, and graph development, and the capability to create form styles and associated actions that PowerMaker developers can use to create forms without programming. The Enterprise Edition comes with a Powersoft native database interface (the user can select which one) and a set of ODBC drivers. It includes the Watcom RDBMS.

PowerMaker relies on predefined form styles and actions. It comes with the same tools for repository and database management and for query, report, and graph development as PowerBuilder. However, it includes additional ODBC drivers plus a functional subset of each of the native database interfaces Powersoft offers. Similar to PowerBuilder, it is bundled with the Watcom RDBMS engine.

However, the two take different approaches to OOP. PowerBuilder follows the OOP paradigm which allows for code reuse, while PowerMaker exploits the benefits of OOP without giving designers access to OOP tools for enhancing its canned styles.

Figure 10.3 illustrates Powersoft's Enterprise series.

Foundation for Cooperative Processing (FCP) Version 2.0 – *from Andersen Consulting, which has local offices in most countries around the world.*

FCP has an object-based LAN repository which allows users to create reusable objects down to the level of individual data names. FCP 2.0 is said to blend traditional CASE-style, front-end tools with faster object-oriented aids very well.

Figure 10.3 Inside Powersoft's Enterprise Series

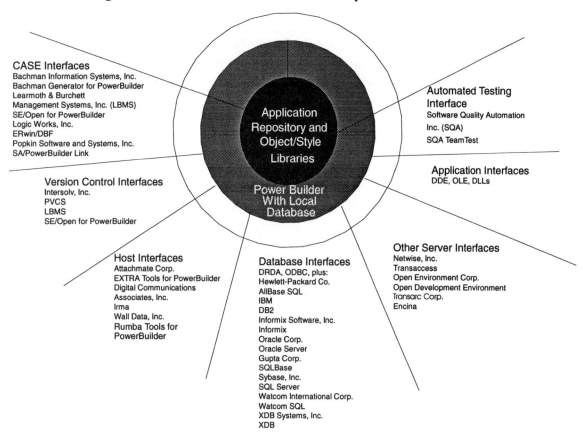

CASE Interfaces
Bachman Information Systems, Inc.
Bachman Generator for PowerBuilder
Learmoth & Burchett
Management Systems, Inc. (LBMS)
SE/Open for PowerBuilder
Logic Works, Inc.
ERwin/DBF
Popkin Software and Systems, Inc.
SA/PowerBuilder Link

Version Control Interfaces
Intersolv, Inc.
PVCS
LBMS
SE/Open for PowerBuilder

Host Interfaces
Attachmate Corp.
EXTRA Tools for PowerBuilder
Digital Communications
Associates, Inc.
Irma
Wall Data, Inc.
Rumba Tools for
PowerBuilder

Database Interfaces
DRDA, ODBC, plus:
Hewlett-Packard Co.
AllBase SQL
IBM
DB2
Informix Software, Inc.
Informix
Oracle Corp.
Oracle Server
Gupta Corp.
SQLBase
Sybase, Inc.
SQL Server
Watcom International Corp.
Watcom SQL
XDB Systems, Inc.
XDB

Application Repository and Object/Style Libraries

Power Builder With Local Database

Automated Testing Interface
Software Quality Automation
Inc. (SQA)
SQA TeamTest

Application Interfaces
DDE, OLE, DLLs

Other Server Interfaces
Netwise, Inc.
Transaccess
Open Environment Corp.
Open Development Environment
Transarc Corp.
Encina

Source: Datamation, Powersoft Corp.

FCP 2.0 runs on OS/2 and can generate applications for HP's HP/UX and DEC's Ultrix platforms. FCP 2.0 also includes a Rapid Application Builder so users can prototype and error-check applications before building them.

ObjectView – *from KnowledgeWare, Inc., Atlanta, Georgia. Tel. 404-365-0246.*

ObjectView has non-proprietary scripting options, offers workgroup development, and object-oriented techniques. Support, training, and consulting services are available to guide users through all phases of C/S development.

KnowledgeWare was acquired by Sterling Software, Inc. in December 1994, which leads to some uncertainty about the future of KnowledgeWare's tools – it is not yet clear how these will fit into Sterling's portfolio.

AD/Method for Client/Server and AD/Method for Business Process Reengineering (BPR) – *from Structured Solutions, Inc., Atlanta, Georgia. Tel.: 404-618-7900.*

AD/Method for C/S is a full lifecycle methodology for developing both small-scale and enterprisewide C/S applications. AD/Method for BPR enables users to reexamine and redesign company processes step-by-step at each level of the corporation.

Both products are offered with Structured Solutions' MAP/Administrator, an automated administrative platform which integrates methodology and tools into a multitasking environment.

Borland C++ 4.0 – *Borland International, Inc., Scotts Valley, California. Tel. 408-431-1000.*

Borland C++ 4.0 supports both 16-bit and 32-bit development. It offers visual programming tools including AppExpert which creates sample Microsoft Windows applications, ClassExpert, a built-in Editor, Resource Workshop Integration, a design tool for customizing user interfaces, an integrated GUI debugger, a character-based debugger, Borland's ObjectWindows Library 2.0, high-level controls such as tool bars, status bars, and floating palettes, and API coverage which includes the Microsoft Windows graphical device interface.

Borland C++ 4.0 enables OOP, support for templates, exception handling, runtime-type information, and ANSI strings are also included. Borland C++ 4.0 supports Microsoft Corp.'s VEX controls. It also includes the a control pack that includes 25 VEX custom controls such as database, spreadsheet, graphics, communication, and word processing.

SQLWindows 5.0 – *Gupta Corp., Menlo Park, California. Tel. 415-321-9500.*

SQLWindows 5.0 is the latest release of Gupta's award-winning AD system. It can be used to build multiuser C/S database applications for Microsoft Windows, Windows NT, and OS/2 workstations.

Applications built can range from departmental applications, accessing a LAN database server to enterprisewide mission-critical ones, with hundreds of concurrent users accessing and updating SQL databases on minicomputers and mainframes.

The Application Designer feature of SQLWindows is a visual programming environment for designing application screens, forms, and objects. As programmers add and modify objects in the Application Designer using point-and-click and drag-and-drop techniques, SQLWindows automatically generates the appropriate code and documentation.

In addition to common data types, objects can incorporate images, sound, and video for creating sophisticated multimedia applications. The Application Designer includes:

- A palette of painting and customizing tools;

- Context-sensitive help;

- QuestWindow – an SQL-intelligent application object that allows entry-level programmers use Quest – Gupta graphical data access tool for end-users – to build applications without writing code or knowing SQL. A programmer can drop a QuestWindow, such as a browse-and-edit table or a form-window object, directly into an SQLWindows application and use Quest's point-and-click interface to produce SQL code automatically; and

- TableWindow – a data-intelligent programming power tool which automates data retrieval, display, and updating in tabular form. It is managed by high-level functions and minimizes programming effort. A single function populates a TableWindow with data from a database. Similar functions manage updates, deletions, and insertions.

The Application Outliner is a readable, collapsible outline which provides a complete overall view of application components. It is updated immediately when application objects are added or modified in the Application Designer window. The outline provides a convenient, flexible way of documenting and navigating through large applications, and eases application maintenance and enhancement.

SQLWindows Application Language is a full-featured 4GL for programming custom application actions and object methods. It supports:

- 500 SQLWindows and Microsoft Windows functions;

- The ability to create and share new functions;

- Any back-end datatypes;

- Variables and arrays;

- Complete control flow; and

- Access to externally developed code, including C and C++.

TeamWindows is a data dictionary-driven repository for project metadata and reusable application building blocks. It has repository-based tools to facilitate and support collaborative programming.

TeamWindows enables the sharing and reuse of application components, the enforcement of standards across application projects, and specialization of programming tasks. It also automates administrative tasks such as staffing, security, standards enforcement, and quality control of the development, test, and production environments of an application. In addition, TeamWindows produces continual, up-to-date reports on the status of every phase of an AD project.

Throughout the AD cycle, TeamWindows enables project leaders to manage team members, track application components, and maintain source code at various levels. Its repository stores everything from forms and reports to programming standards and staffing information. This allows fast, consistent, database-aware AD – programmers can implement reusable code across applications rather than rewriting functionally similar code.

TeamWindows is a multiuser repository. It uses a full-function relational database server – initially Gupta SQLBase Server – and enables:

- *Data dictionary-driven application generation.* TeamWindows maintains a central dictionary of database structural information, including table and column names, primary and foreign-key relationships, validation criteria, and other parameters. This data can be imported from existing upper-CASE tools.

- *Impact analysis.* Whenever database structures change or the data dictionary is modified, TeamWindows automatically modifies any affected applications. Reports that track the use of any object can be run.

- *Secure source-code and version control.* Once an SQLWindows application is complete, it can be stored in the repository and managed with the TeamWindows source-code controller.

The check-in/check-out facility allows team members to share and modify application components, while repository security denies access to unauthorized users and ensures that only one programmer can modify a particular component at any one time.

TeamWindows also tracks and automatically updates version numbers for application modules throughout the entire development cycle. TeamWindows provides pre-defined templates for quickly generating SQLWindows screens and applications using data dictionary information. Programmers can also save and reuse screens as templates for new applications across multiple databases.

Gupta Quest is a query and reporting tool, which enables end-users to build ad hoc reports and integrate them into the SQLWindows applications without needing to know SQL or programming.

ReportWindows is an integrated, full-featured graphical report designer and writer. It can produce tabular, cross-tab, and control-break reports to any level of detail, and offers a full selection of fonts, colors, and other formatting options. Reports created with ReportWindows are fully compatible with reports created with Quest.

Gupta SQLBase Server for Windows is a single-user multitasking copy of a full-function SQL database server. It makes SQLWindows ready for development right out of the box. The database also enables application testing and debugging on standalone PCs and laptops.

The SQLWindows debugger enables interactive application refinement and testing using multiple breakpoints, single-stepping, watch values, and code animation. Applications can then be compiled into a compact and efficient executable form for deployment on multiple workstations. SQLWindows' utilities include tools for database administration, library browsing, and for customizing and translating applications to national languages.

SQLWindows tools and applications use the full power of the Microsoft Windows environment. Both the Application Designer and SQL Application Language support dynamic data exchange (DDE), OLE, multiple document interface (MDI), and external dynamic link libraries (DLL). Also, any Windows message call can be used in SQL Windows.

TeamWindows offers team coordination and management capabilities required for collaborative programming. Many of these were only found on previous minicomputers and mainframes. They include:

- Project management and reporting;

- Automatic application generation and impact analysis;

- Secure, repository-based source code, and version control; and

- Configuration management.

New features in SQLWindows 5.0 include QuickObjects, workgroup integration, and a 4GL compiler. QuickObjects is an architecture which provides a suite of easy-to-learn reusable components. These allow even new C/S developers to quickly assemble object-oriented applications.

SQLWindows 5.0 provides three kinds of QuickObjects: QuickObject Data Sources, which control the interaction between applications and data, enabling easy and consistent access to both SQL and non-SQL data; QuickObject Visualizers, which control the presentation of data to users, facilitating maximum flexibility in display of data; and QuickObject Commanders, which direct user commands to QuickObject Data Sources, making it easy to manipulate data.

QuickObjects are both extensible and maintainable because they are built on the object-oriented foundation of SQLWindows. New QuickObjects can be created and integrated seamlessly into the SQLWindows development environment.

Because QuickObjects support relational and non-relational data sources, they can be used to create applications that draw on data sources such as those contained in Lotus Notes or any leading electronic mail package. Developers can build applications which draw from a variety of data sources and provide more enterprisewide integration by choosing the appropriate QuickObject Data Source and assigning Visualizers and Commanders to that source.

Finally, the SQLWindows Compiler converts 4GL code to C code. This increases AD speed by up to 200%. To use the SQLWindows Compiler, developers write the application using SQLWindows, invoke the SQLWindows Compiler, then run the accelerated application.

When SQLWindows code is converted into C code, it is automatically converted into a DLL (see Figure 10.4). The DLL is seamlessly linked with the SQLWindows application. The C DLL generated is fully functional and does not require any changes. It includes support for communicating back with the SQLWindows code and interacting with local and remote databases.

Figure 10.4 SQL Windows Application

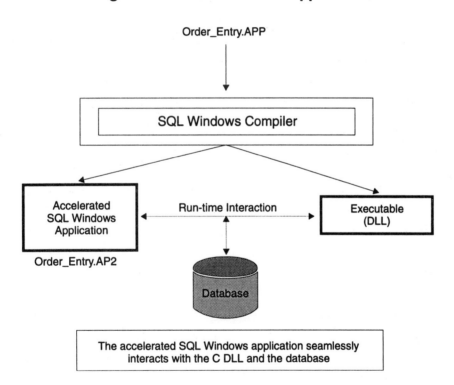

Gain Momentum 2.0 – *from Sybase, Inc., Emeryville, California. Tel. 510-596-3500.*

This is an object-oriented multimedia development environment which combines a user interface with seamless integrated access to RDBMSs. It is targeted at "extended office" applications which require an information-rich user interface to entice both internal users, such as executives and outside users – customers – to interact with the corporation's computer system.

Gain Momentum 2.0 consists of integrated visual development tools for creating, importing, and editing multimedia data objects such as text, graphics, images, audio, video, and special effects.

Developers can establish libraries of reusable components by interactively creating objects and defining their properties through point-and-click dialogs. These libraries are automatically stored and managed in a built-in object-oriented database.

Application behavior is created by writing scripts in the Gain Momentum 4GL. Gain Momentum 2.0 also incorporates tools for establishing connections to multiple SQL database servers and for presenting SQL data within interactive multimedia applications.

Version 2.0 of Gain Momentum is available on the Sun Sparc, IBM AIX, HP/UX workstation platforms, and on Microsoft Windows NT.

Build Momentum *– from Sybase, Inc., Emeryville, California 94608. Tel. 510-596-3500.*

Build Momentum is a graphical, object-oriented environment for deploying and developing applications on Microsoft Windows, Windows NT, Apple Macintosh, and OSF/Motif platforms.

It is targeted at the front office which is characterized by graphical, management-oriented, and real-time decision support applications. Build Momentum speeds the development of high-performance C/S applications for GUI-based desktop platforms used in transaction-intensive business processes such as financials, materials resource planning (MRP), reservations, and ticketing.

Applications developed in Build Momentum emphasize speed and efficiency in accessing and manipulating transaction-oriented data from leading relational database servers, including Sybase SQL Server, Oracle, and DB2.

Build Momentum uses a 32-bit internal architecture which expands the capabilities of C/S applications, even when they run on 16-bit platforms. For example, a Build Momentum application running under Microsoft Windows on an 80486 PC can handle multitasking functions.

Another feature is built-in automatic performance tuning. During runtime, Build Momentum dynamically monitors application performance characteristics and continually adjusts to achieve the optimal relationship between speed and memory use. It maximizes application performance while preserving memory for other applications which may be critical to user productivity by compiling only the most frequently used application functions to machine code.

Sybase customers will be able to move applications created with APT Workbench, Sybase's previous development tool, into Build Momentum which supports the APT-SQL language.

Enterprise Momentum – *from Sybase, Inc., Emeryville, California. Tel. 510-596-3500.*

Enterprise Momentum is an object-oriented development framework based on an active repository for building complex, enterprisewide applications. It consists of Enterprise Modelers, the Enterprise Meta Server, and Enterprise Application Builders. The Meta Server is the repository.

Enterprise modelers are used to create, access, and browse through the data application objects within the repository. They integrate process modeling, data modeling, and user interface modeling to give developers insight into the entire business information lifecycle.

Enterprise Meta Server is the key link between the models and their representative applications. It extends the model definitions by storing their associated business rules. Many of these rules are defined through a declarative, point-and-click interface. This reduces the need for writing traditional code.

Enterprise Momentum contains an integrated application builder which directly translates stored models into executable applications.

Enterprise Momentum is based on an open architecture and will work with third-party development tools, CASE products, heterogeneous databases, and data sources.

Sybase will move its Deft CASE product into Enterprise Momentum, and its Build Momentum and Gain Momentum tools will work as application builders in the Enterprise Momentum environment.

NeXTStep Developer Release 3 – *from Next Computer, Inc., Redwood City, California. Tel. 415-366-0900.*

NeXTStep Developer provides a complete development environment for NeXTStep, the leader in object-oriented operating systems, which runs on both NeXT hardware and computers based on the Intel 80486 and Pentium central processing units (CPUs).

NeXTStep comes with the following development tools:

- *Project Builder* – the central application for building, debugging, and managing software projects.

  It manages all files and resources associated with an application, generates Makefiles, and provides a graphical interface to the MAKE command. It also allows developers to go immediately from a compiler error to the line in the editor where the error occurred by clicking on the error message.

- *Interface Builder* – a rapid prototyping tool and object editor which enables developers to design the relationship between objects in an application.

  It includes a user interface layout tool and facilities for subclassing existing objects. Interface Builder also provides graphical palettes for NeXT Object Kits. In addition, it lets developers load third-party or custom-made palettes of objects not supplied by NeXT.

- *Edit* – a powerful, integrated, mouse-oriented graphical editor for code and online help. It can be used to create help files which contain graphics and hypertext-like links.

- *Graphical Debugger* – offers easy graphical access to debugging. It includes the ability to debug optimized code and data breakpoints. The debugger is fully integrated with Edit and Project Builder. Other features include mouse access to setting breakpoints, the capability to examine data, and other graphical debugger features. It also includes a data browser which lets developers explore the current execution stack and its local variables.

- *MallocDebug* – a tool for measuring dynamic memory usage of the application being built. This is useful for detecting memory leaks.

- *Header Viewer* – a class browser for navigating object class hierarchies, providing access to class information and documentation. It navigates the NeXT Object Kits and application code developed by users.

- *DBModeler* – a graphical tool for building data models. It was specifically designed for use with Database Kit, and enables users to build and customize data models based on the data dictionary of an underlying database.

- *Yap* – an interactive PostScript language previewer for entering and executing PostScript code, making it easier to debug.

- *Icon Builder* – a simple, pixel-based editor for creating icons.

- *Application Kit* – a rich set of standard objects which provide the framework for all applications with a variety of customization options. It includes a complete set of user interface controls and objects, and objects that support data sharing and inter-application communication.

Look and feel is consistent across all NeXTStep applications. Application Kit objects provide a standard framework for handling details such as event management, window management, printing, and fax capability. Because all of NeXT's kits consist of Objective C objects, users can modify or extend their behavior through subclassing.

Data sharing features such as Cut, Copy, and Paste are automatically supported between all applications. More advanced features such as live-links and inter-application services can be easily integrated into the application. Distributed Objects make it easy to implement C/S applications.

NeXTStep Developer comes bundled with the Objective C, ANSI C, PostScript Level II, and C++ languages. It also offers online help, multiarchitecture binary support, and source code compatibility across all NeXTStep platforms.

db-UIM/X – from Bluestone Communications, Inc., Mount Laurel, New Jersey. Tel. 609-727-4600.

This product is an object-oriented development tool for building OSF/Motif-based C/S applications. It is optimized for accessing RDBMSs.

Bluestone's db-UIM/X extends the capabilities of the leading GUI builder in the Motif market – Visual Edge Software, Inc.'s User Interface Management for X Systems (UIM/X), which is resold by IBM, Bluestone and HP. Bluestone db-UIM/X lets developers use the UIM/X front-end, point-and-click GUI builder to update and retrieve data stored on Sybase SQL Server RDBMSs.

This product allows developers to treat SQL Server-stored procedures as objects which can interact dynamically with GUI objects through an ORB. Bluestone's db-UIM/X supports an end-to-end, distributed, object computing environment.

Developers need not learn a new programming or scripting language. All actions, including binding a GUI object to a remotely stored procedure, are done through a point-and-click interface. However, db-UIM/X, which is written in C and C++, gives users the option of writing code in those languages.

Bluestone claims its ORB is compliant with the OMG CORBA. The ORB, which can reside anywhere on a TCP/IP network, manages the exchange of information between client and server objects.

Communications between clients, ORBs, and servers are handled by RPCs which are compatible with the OSF's DCE. The RPCs, along with a proprietary queuing mechanism, offer both synchronous and asynchronous communications between clients and servers.

dBase for Windows – *from Borland International, Inc., Scotts Valley, California. Tel. 408-438-8400.*

This offers true Microsoft Windows compatibility. It also comes with object-oriented dBase extensions, a scalable database engine, and object-oriented development tools. The package uses event-driven methodology.

Object Inspectors provide users with the option to view and modify dBase window, tool and object properties, while the OOP extensions and the event-driven model provide object-oriented features such as inheritance, polymorphism, and encapsulation. dBase for Windows ships with 20 predefined object classes.

A new two-way tools feature enables programmers to make changes in one code form and have the change reflected in the other. For example, if a change is made in visual code, it is interpreted and presented in the dBase source code. Programmers can make changes in both environments in realtime without duplicating their efforts. Nothing will get lost in translation.

Borland offers SQL Links for Windows drivers dBase to its for Windows buyers. These offer the ability to connect to back-end database servers from Oracle Corp. and Informix Software, Inc., and to the SQL Server provided jointly by Sybase, Inc. and Microsoft Corp.

Object-oriented Analysis & Design Pilot Bundle – *from Bernard Software Engineering, Gaithersburg, Maryland. Tel. 301-417-9884.*

This product includes an object-oriented CASE tool, user documentation, a publication on object-oriented design, and selected slides from an object-oriented training course.

The CASE tool allows users to create programming language-independent object specifications and generates formatted documents combining text and graphics. It is limited to saving 15 models and 15 object specifications.

Smalltalk/V and PARTS – *from Digitalk, Inc., Santa Ana, California. Tel. 714-513-3000.*

Digitalk is best known for its inexpensive version of the Smalltalk OOP language. Smalltalk/V is targeted toward application component developers. It insulates programmers from complex systems and structures, so they are free to create applications to solve business and production problems.

The Smalltalk/V series consists of a complete, object-oriented development environment for developing graphical, portable applications. It includes automatic memory management, browsers, debuggers, other tools, and Smalltalk source code.

Smalltalk/V is available on several platforms:

- Smalltalk/V for OS/2 – a 32-bit version fully integrated with OS/2 2.x;

- Smalltalk/V for Win32 – a 32-bit version for Microsoft Windows 3.x and Windows NT;

- Smalltalk/V for Windows – a 16-bit version running on Microsoft Windows 3.x for entry-level programmers; and

- Smalltalk/V for Macintosh – fully integrated with Macintosh System 7.

Digitalk also offers the Team/V series. Products in this series organize the work of a team of Smalltalk/V developers by providing a programming environment through which large programming teams can structure and coordinate their work. They support and include Intersolv's industry standard PVCS Version Manager. There are two products in the Team/V series: Team/V for Smalltalk/V for OS/2 and Team/V for Smalltalk/V for Win32.

Digitalk's Parts Assembly and Reuse Tool Set (PARTS) series is targeted at application part integrators and enables rapid application from prefabricated software parts. The product is based on Smalltalk/V OT. The PARTS technology is language-neutral to the user, so no knowledge of Smalltalk/V is required. This also allows PARTS technology to integrate components from other languages.

PARTS technology lets users develop applications much faster because it shields them from the complexity of both the OS and the components. This allows users to concentrate on their development work. Each part has a common interface, so once a part has been created, it can be assembled more quickly into a finished application than is possible using conventional technologies. IBM has deemed Digitalk PARTS to be a complementary technology to Smalltalk/V in IBM's AD/Cycle strategy.

PARTS Workbench is the first in a series of PARTS products. It is a complete AD environment and enables point-and-click, graphical assembly and interconnection of parts.

PARTS enables developers to create many applications without programming. The PARTS Workbench comes with more than 60 ready-to-use visual and non-visual application parts. It also reduces development time by eliminating the compile-link-run loop used in non-OOP languages.

Visual parts include components that conform to IBM's common user access (CUA) standards. These include notebook, value set, container, horizontal and vertical sliders, push buttons, drop-down list, menu, text pane, check box, multiple choice list, picture field, static graphic, and window.

Non-visual parts provide the data access, computation and other services for the applications built. These parts include a Btrieve database file accesser, several data structure parts, DDE client and server connections, DLL accesser, disk accesser, file accesser, printer, file system interface, and external program launch pad.

New parts can be created visually with the PARTS Workbench or modified with the built-in PARTStalk scripting language. Users can also create parts with Smalltalk/V, C, C++, and other development languages. This lets users leverage their investment in existing technology. Parts are easily integrated and interchanged as files.

Chapter 11

Application Development Tools

There are many GUI and network application tools on the market in various areas of AD.

Tips for Developing Great Graphical User Interfaces

Developing GUIs is extremely difficult for those coming from procedural programming backgrounds such as COBOL who must learn a whole new way of thinking. Here are some tips to help developers create better GUIs:

- *Less-used information should be shunted-off onto subwindows.*

  Developers need not fit all the fields onto one window as they do with a 3270 terminal screen. Instead, they can put pick lists, messages, and field-dependent information onto subwindows. This makes for a less cluttered, more usable window. It is the same principle as good layout in publishing – properly used white space makes for an uncluttered, clean look and feel, and is more inviting than a crowded, crammed page or window.

- *Windows should be kept clean.*

  Too many shapes and objects or too many colors will be visually disturbing and offensive to the user's eye. Screen objects should be balanced with white space.

- *Consistency in design is important.*

  The same font and size should be used for related buttons. Also, the actions to invoke subroutines using the buttons should be the same for related buttons. This will make the program easier to learn and to develop.

- *Developers should determine what users will use.*

  The aim of creating an application is to design one users will want to use. Putting in too many objects will deter users. Take Microsoft Windows, for example: few users actually use all the buttons and functions available on the screen.

- *Developers should use a whiteboard to draw screen designs rather than prototyping in the GUI environment.*

  Hand-drawing two or three versions of the most important screens is faster than prototyping. Also, if things must be changed, it is easier to alter drawings than code. This further helps to ensure programmers do not get attached to designs, which are not quite optimal to justify the amount of time they spent in prototyping.

- *The user should be taken into consideration.*

  To make the user happy, encourage use of the application and make the screen easier to view. The number of fonts and font sizes should be limited to three or four per window. Italics and serif fonts should not be used because they tend to break up on the screen. Also, neutral colors should be used for the background.

- *Keyboard controls for the screen should be included in the design.*

  If no allowance is made for keyboard control, things will come to a halt when the mouse breaks down. Also, many users prefer to mix keyboard and mouse shortcuts, especially to avoid repetitive strain injuries (for example, carpal tunnel syndrome). Bear in mind that, even though the Apple Macintosh was designed for mouse use, Macintosh power users are those who know how to take and use keyboard shortcuts.

- *Create and implement a naming standard.*

GUI systems tend to have numerous modules and objects, and many of these must be modified when a name is changed. This makes things much more complex, and can waste valuable time.

Cross-Platform Tools Gain Popularity

Things were easier when C/S systems were seen as good only for departmental computing: most departments standardized on one GUI. As more organizations opt for C/S environments, the number of hardware platforms is increasing. Support for multiple GUIs and even character interfaces is required, and tools which allow users to develop and deploy applications in multiple environments are becoming increasingly important.

Vendors are providing cross-platform graphical development capabilities in three ways. One method is the superset approach – offering the greatest common denominator for all the graphical environments. Tools from vendors taking this approach offer a common look and feel and similar functionality across the graphical environments they serve. The second is to provide true native capabilities in each environment. The third method is to offer GUI extensions on top of native look and feel.

For example, Neuron Data, Inc. of Palo Alto, California offers a family of four GUI design tools. The latest, Smart Elements, offers the superset approach to cross-platform implementation. It consists of a set of libraries which convert calls or instructions to the operating systems of various computers. Users can see how an application would look in the new environment before deploying it. Neuron Data supports UNIX, Microsoft Windows and Windows NT, Apple Macintosh, OS/2 PM, OpenVMS for Alpha and DOS, and VMS character mode. Databases supported include Sybase, Oracle, Ingres, Informix, Microsoft's ODBC, and Neuron Data NXPDB. The product also provides platform emulation.

An example of a firm taking the native windows approach is XVT Software, Inc., of Boulder, Colorado. Its XVT Portability Toolkit supports Microsoft Windows, Windows NT, Apple Macintosh, OS/2, OSF/Motif, Sun Open Look, and character systems for MS-DOS, UNIX and VMS. It uses the native toolkits for each windowing environment to provide native look and feel.

XVT's argument is that emulation, taken in the superset approach, may compromise application performance and native look and feel. Its development solution is implemented as a thin layer on top of the native GUI API which gives access to native functionality without overloading an application's performance or increasing its size.

One firm offering the third approach – GUI extensions on top of native look and feel – is Sapiens USA, Inc., of Research Triangle Park, North Carolina. It offers cross-platform capability across Microsoft Windows, OSF/Motif, and Apple Macintosh. Sapiens' approach is to take the least common denominator of each environment and expand it. Its Ideo product provides enhanced objects if a facility is not available in a windowing environment.

For example, the GUI feature Combo Boxes, which is offered in Microsoft Windows, is an enhanced object in OSF/Motif. Ideo supports access to Ingres, Sybase, Oracle, Informix, and Rdb.

Graphical/Graphical User Interface Development Tools

Visual Baler 1.0 – *from Baler Software Corp., Rolling Meadows, Illinois. Tel. 708-506-9700.*

This product is a spreadsheet development tool which lets users develop analytical and number-crunching graphical applications based on existing spreadsheet files. Visual Baler 1.0 automatically generates a spreadsheet application which includes a title screen and a program icon.

The application framework includes pre-built routines for functions such as "file open," "save," and "print." Knowledge of programming languages is not necessary.

Cross-Platform Toolset – *from Visual Edge Software, Ltd., St.-Laurent, Quebec, Canada. Tel. 514-332-6430.*

Available for HP's HP/UX, Sun Microsystems, Inc.'s SunOS, and Solaris platforms, with application deployment on Microsoft Windows 3.1, the Cross-Platform Toolset provides the objects, libraries, and documentation needed to develop applications for multiple platforms.

The Cross-Platform Toolset is built on native tool kit controls so the ported application interface looks and behaves similar to an application written to the native GUI.

To deploy an application developed with the Cross-Platform Toolset, the developer need only recompile and re-link the code with each platform's object library. Support for Microsoft Windows NT, the Macintosh, and OS/2 platforms were released in late 1994.

WinRPC 2.0 – *from NobleNet, Inc., Southborough, Massachusetts. Tel. 508-460-8222.*

NobleNet's WinRPC 2.0 is a tool which makes building Microsoft Windows-based C/S applications easier. It is a compiler that generates RPCs which bind Windows clients to UNIX and Novell NetWare servers across TCP/IP networks.

WinRPC 2.0 conforms to the WinSock TCP/IP interface. WinSock is an interface between Windows applications and TCP/IP network transport software which was developed by a vendor consortium. It has been implemented by more than 20 TCP/IP vendors, including Frontier Technologies, Inc. and NetManage, Inc.

Two types of RPCs are generated by WinRPC 2.0. One is an RPC for SunSoft, Inc.'s NFS. The other is the Transport Independent RPC which comes bundled with Novell NetWare 3.11, NetWare 4.0, and UNIX System V Release 4.

The RPCs are generated in the form of DLLs which can be called from any Windows program or any high-level visual programming language such as Microsoft's Visual Basic or Powersoft Corp.'s PowerBuilder.

VX-Rexx 2.1 – *from Watcom International, Waterloo, Ontario, Canada. Tel. 519-886-3700.*

As a visual application builder for OS/2, this product offers customization of object properties, multithreading of object properties, multithreading support, object-oriented GUI runtime support, drag-and-drop programming, application integration, and an interactive debugger.

VX-Rexx Client/Server Edition 2.1 – *from Watcom International, Waterloo, Ontario, Canada. Tel. 519-886-3700.*

Also a visual application builder for OS/2, this product incorporates database objects and allows users to visually generate and test SQL series. It has charting capabilities, including support for 12 chart types with more than 150 display options.

DataViews 9.5 – *from V.I. Corp., Northampton, Massachusetts. Tel. 413-586-4144.*

DataViews 9.5 is a programming tool which enables users to build animated graphics to monitor and control real-time processes. Release 9.5 features Motif Object Dynamics, a software tool which enables OSF Motif developers to seamlessly integrate the animated graphics into Motif interfaces.

Users can also construct fully-animated interfaces for analyzing, visualizing, and regulating real-time financial or industrial processes. This eliminates complex coding, and V.I. Corp. claims it can reduce development time by up to 80%.

TeleUse Release 3 – *from Alsys, Inc., San Diego, California. Tel. 619-457-2700.*

TeleUse Release 3 is a GUI development environment which supports C, C++ and user interface languages and large development efforts. It generates true object-oriented C++ code so users can create objects with attributes and methods easily adapted to current and future applications. Developers can drag graphical objects from a visual library and create higher-level objects which reflect business processes.

TeleUse has three components: VIP, Dialog Manager, and user interface Builder. VIP provides GUI components, Dialog Manager manages dynamic components, and user interface Builder administers the building process.

VisualWare for Windows – *from InterGroup Technologies, Bellevue, Washington. Tel. 206-643-8089.*

An embeddable GUI builder for independent software vendors and corporate developers, VisualWare consists of a GUI builder, script editor/debuggers, and an information window. Users can view or change all properties in the design phase.

The GUI builder supports all Microsoft Windows controls, including list boxes, scroll bars, push buttons, and pictures. The script editor allows users to edit their scripts, set breakpoints, and view variables associated with the script. VisualWare enables developers to drag-and-drop graphical objects onto forms.

A menu lets users create custom controls. VisualWare is compatible with Basic and any event-driven language, including COBOL, Fortran, and C. Coupled with a Basic scripting language from another vendor, such as Softbridge, Inc. or Summit Software Co., it will give developers a complete common macro language architecture similar to Microsoft Corp.'s Visual Basic for Applications.

Visual Basic – *from Microsoft Corp., Redmond, Washington. Tel. 206-882-8080.*

Introduced in 1991, Visual Basic is considered a lightweight tool which builds applications that only run under Microsoft Windows. It includes an editor, a compiler, and a debugger.

The Sacramento Municipal Utility District (SMUD), which provides electricity to almost 500,000 consumers in Sacramento, California, began a C/S pilot project in 1991, in which Visual Basic was used to build an energy-usage tracking system running on Windows clients. By 1992, 50 SMUD workers were using the program to access SMUD's Sybase DBMS which ran on a Sun Microsystems SparcStation 10 server.

There are problems with Visual Basic, however. SMUDS said the package is not well-suited to large programming teams – when more than one programmer works with an application, software is needed to track different versions. (This problem can be resolved by putting in an electronic software distribution package or using Microsoft's SMS which will have version control and version tracking features.)

VSVBX 3.0 – *from VideoSoft, in Berkeley, California. Tel. 510-547-7295.*

VSVBX 3.0 contains three controls which enhance Visual Basic: IndexTab, Elastic, and AWK.

IndexTab provides a notebook interface to Visual Basic applications. It can change the position, front and back tab color, style, and more. Tabs are created and labeled by separating them with the pipe character (|) within the caption string.

Elastic is a container that, when resized, can automatically resize its contents. Users can create Visual Basic visually pleasing forms at any resolution. Elastic's most significant property is AutoSize Children. This lets users control the relative size and position of objects contained in Elastic at runtime. To use Elastic effectively, containers must often be nested inside each other.

AWK is the name of a UNIX text processing utility familiar to users. In VSVBX, AWK encapsulates a set of text processing facilities similar to those of UNIX's AWK. It allows fast scanning of text files for specific words and strings. Each text line can contain up to 64 kilobytes of data. AWK is good for building Visual Basic applications such as E-mail managers and file browsers which need to scan multiple files for characters, strings, and words.

MultiLink/VB – *from Q+E Software, Inc., Raleigh, North Carolina.*

MultiLink/VB, a C/S AD tool for Microsoft Corp.'s Visual Basic, gives corporate developers a way to link client applications written in Visual Basic with data stored in SQL databases.

Q+E has enhanced MultiLink/VB with support for Microsoft Corp.'s ODBC standard. This is a widely supported implementation of the SQL Access Group standard.

Analytic Technologies, Inc. of San Diego, California plans to move from Oracle Corp.'s SQLForms applications to MultiLink/VB. It has about 420 users in seven locations running Visual Basic and SQLForms under Windows and accessing the same data in an Oracle database.

The move to MultiLink/VB is being made because Analytic Technologies feels this will reduce the work associated with direct access to a SQL database by about 70%. MultiLink/VB is robust enough for Analytic Technologies to incorporate a horizontal scroll capability into its applications.

Visual M – *from InterSystems Corp., Cambridge, Massachusetts. Tel. 617-621-0600.*

Visual M is based on a combination of Microsoft Corp.'s Visual Basic and the M language which is ANSI-standard. It is part of InterSystem's "GUI of Choice" product which offers alternative GUI development environments for high-volume C/S applications.

Vaps 3.1 – *from Virtual Prototypes, Inc., Montreal, Quebec, Canada. Tel: 514-341-3874.*

Vaps 3.1 is a toolset for automating the building and deployment of real-time graphical interfaces. Interfaces created with Vaps enables users to interact with the application through graphical representations of real-world objects.

Users develop the interfaces with a set of editors supporting an object-oriented approach. Vaps 3.1 automatically translates the graphical prototypes into C code.

APS for Client/Server – *from Intersolv, Inc., Rockville, Maryland. Tel. 301-230-3200.*

APS for C/S is a GUI-based software package enabling teams of developers to generate OS/2 and Microsoft Windows client applications. It includes multiple document interfaces, user-configurable toolbars, and floating tool palettes. Applications generated can access IBM host databases through IBM's Advanced Program-to-Program Communications (APPC) protocol.

The use of APPC makes APS for C/S scalable because APPC provides direct access to host-based systems which many companies still use to handle mission-critical TP applications.

APS for C/S simplifies the process of using APPC by mapping APPC calls directly into APS' specification language. Application developers need not learn the complexities of APPC. Performance gains because third-party gateways are not required to access legacy systems. Many other C/S AD tools require third-party gateways.

The downside to APPC mapping is it takes a great deal of time to reconfigure communications controllers, operating systems, and transaction monitors to run APPC, especially if there are no APPC experts in-house. It is also a very complex task.

Valero Energy Corp. of San Antonio, Texas used APS for C/S to develop an OS/2 application which accesses IBMs DB2 relational database on an MVS/CICS server. Developers built a prototype C/S application with APS, but it took nine months to implement. Despite this, Valero thinks the project was worthwhile because performance is excellent and it is designed to implement other C/S applications quickly.

APS for C/S also generates applications which can access relational databases from IBM, Oracle Corp., and Sybase, Inc. running on both UNIX and PCs. One of its major new features is Client Express. This is a point-and-click tool enabling developers on OS/2 or Windows PCs to rapidly generate C/S applications without writing code.

Developers can toggle out of Client Express to APS' high-level specification language based on SQL to extend the development environment to meet special application, communications or data access requirements. For even greater control, an APS macro language can be used to change the rules on which the APS graphical environment is based. This minimizes the need for developers to go to C to customize a program.

APS for C/S can be integrated with Intersolv's other software development tools – Excelerator, PVCS and Maintenance Workbench – to provide a comprehensive C/S application design and maintenance environment. It does not require users to buy proprietary run-time modules to generate executable code because applications generated are a composite of APPC or TCP/IP code, SQL, and industry-standard COBOL.

The product supports all C/S topologies, including distributed presentation, distributed function, and remote/distributed data management. APS for C/S supports the OS/2 PM, and Microsoft Windows on the client side, and UNIX, Microsoft Windows, and Microsoft Windows NT on the server side.

APS for C/S runs on Windows and OS/2 machines. It generates Windows and OS/2 client programs, OS/2, MVS, and CICS server programs, and MVS batch processes.

Databases supported are IBM's DB2, DB2/2, DB2/6000, SQL/400, IMS, VSAM, Oracle Corp.'s Oracle Server Sybase, Inc.'s SQL Server.

CA-Visual Realia – *from Computer Associates International, Inc., Islandia, New York. Tel. 516-342-5224.*

This is a graphical development system which uses COBOL as its procedural business language, giving developers the best of both worlds. Users enjoy the ease-of-use of the GUI/icon/toolbar/DLL paradigm and the power, flexibility, and familiarity of COBOL.

CA-Visual Realia is closely related to CA-Realia II Workbench, a PC-based AD tool suite for developing and maintaining character-based COBOL applications, typically for IBM mainframes, UNIX, and other mainframe and midrange platforms. It contains all the technology available in CA-Realia II Workbench, except that which is specifically related to character-based programs.

A full COBOL workbench permits seamless adaptation of legacy code into CA-Visual Realia applications. The workbench can also be used by trained COBOL programmers to write new COBOL functions as part of GUI applications.

The look and feel of native Microsoft Windows is offered, and CA-Visual Realia has a graphical form painter. To use the form painter, developers drag-and-drop controls onto the form, then set or modify the control's properties by filling in blanks or, for complex functionality, COBOL coding.

A powerful set of custom controls is available in CA-Visual Realia. In addition to widgets, floating toolbars, and other normal controls, it has container controls for creating complex application behavior.

Analysis tools provided are COBOL-oriented and COBOL-aware with flow diagrams and tree diagrams. CA-Visual Realia also has an integrated debugging tool with seamless single-stepping between the interpreted pseudo-code of the GUI functions and the compiled COBOL of the application logic.

CA-Visual Realia has a strong project management workbench with installation generation facilities. The Installation Manager goes beyond compiling, linking, and packaging to automatically create a full set of installation functions and procedures. This is tied together through a project management paradigm.

CA-Visual Realia is fully event-driven. The business logic, which is executed in response to events such as menu selections, button clicks or data entry is written in standard procedural COBOL code with standard database operations. It has a rich set of proprietary custom controls.

When it comes to DBMS support, CA-Visual Realia can embed any dialect of SQL. It supports any RDBMS with an SQL pre-compiler, including CA-OpenIngres, CA-Datacom, CA-IDMS, Oracle, and DB2. Support for ODBC lets CA-Visual Realia access borderline DBMSs such as groupware systems and PC databases.

Platforms currently supported are Microsoft Windows and IBM OS/2.

CA-DBFast/400 – *from Computer Associates International, Inc., Islandia, New York. Tel. 516-342-5224.*

CA-DBFast/400 claims to be the first intuitive GUI C/S development tool for IBM AS/400 users. It can be used to develop Microsoft Windows C/S applications which can immediately access AS/400-based data and communicate with and enhance AS/400 systems.

The life of character-based AS/400 code can be extended by using CA-DBFast/400 to add GUI C/S application functionality. Programmers can create AS/400 applications with minimal training. Program logic can execute on both the AS/400 and PCs running Microsoft Windows. Graphical design tools simplify the creation of custom applications with pull-down menus, radio buttons, check boxes, resizeable windows, mouse support, icons, video, and other Windows GUI attributes.

The major features of CA-DBFast/400 are:

- Communication with other Microsoft Windows and AS/400 programs because the full support for DDE and DLL allows CA-DBFast/400 applications to tie into current code with full two-way communications.

- Visual reporting – advanced WYSIWYG desktop reporting gives users the ability to easily produce complex, visually appealing reports.

- Minimal coding – graphical design tools, screen and report painters, and an integrated data dictionary minimize and simplify program code.

- Full AS/400 security – access validation and file selection criteria ensure compliance with standard OS/400 security.

- RPCs – remote AS/400 programs can be invoked with parameters passed, including automated ASCII to EBCDIC translation.

- Source-code generation – full source-code representing client-side applications can be generated in native CA-DBFast/400 code at any point in the development cycle.

RadPath – *from Corporate Computing, Inc., Bannockburn, Illinois. Tel. 708-374-1995.*

RadPath is a development methodology providing online checklists to ensure consistent software development processes. It is designed to help organizations develop GUI C/S applications.

There are three components of RadPath – infrastructure, management, and development. These functional components are designed to define optional and required tasks. RadPath runs under Microsoft Windows 3.1 and can run standalone or on a LAN.

ToolBook 3.0 – *a visual programming application, and*
Multimedia ToolBook 3.0 *– a multimedia authoring system. From Asymetrix Corp., Bellevue, Washington. Tel. 206-426-0501.*

These products were designed for visual software developers of front-ends and prototypes; authors of computer-based training, hypermedia and information kiosk applications, and CD-ROM publishers.

ToolBook 3.0 contains a book metaphor and object-orientation to provide an environment for the development of interactive applications. Multimedia ToolBook 3.0 has the same features, but it adds a multimedia engine, path-based animation, and full-motion video editing.

Axiant *– from Cognos, Inc., Ottawa, Ontario, Canada. Sales, service, and marketing: Tel. 617-229-6600.*

A second-generation C/S toolset, Axiant offers users an architecture for building, deploying, and maintaining complex enterprise C/S applications. It provides an integrated, visual development environment built around a multiuser, object-oriented repository running under Microsoft Windows. All application logic is described using a powerful, non-procedural scripting language.

The first phase runs on Intel platforms running Microsoft Windows with UNIX, Intel, DOS, and DEC VAX/VMS servers. Phase Two will support IBM AS/400 and HP MPE iX servers.

PowerBuilder *– from Powersoft Corp., Burlington, Massachusetts. Tel. 617-229-2200.*

PowerBuilder is believed to be the market leader for PC-based C/S AD tools. Key benefits are ease-of-development and the ability for users to use prototyping.

The Northern Trust Corp., a bank holding company based in Chicago, used PowerBuilder to create new front-ends for retail banking, mortgage, and other business applications in less than nine months. It plans to have 100 developers use PowerBuilder to write programs over the next few years.

On the other hand, Amoco Canada Petroleum Co., a Calgary, Canada-based subsidiary of oil firm Amoco Corp., is not quite so keen on PowerBuilder. In early 1992, Amoco Canada decided to move a mainframe application that tracked oil and gas well usage to UNIX workstations using PowerBuilder. The tool allowed programmers to build the application without extensive training.

However, the applications could not generate complex reports. In many cases, Amoco Canada relies on C programs rather than PowerBuilder for its reports.

In recent months, Powersoft has been heavily criticized by users because of bugs in its PowerBuilder 3.0 C/S development toolset. Some users on CompuServe's Powersoft forum have described system failures occurring with Powersoft's debugger, screen and database painters, and when Powersoft is used with some video monitors. Some developers say they lose 10% to 20% of development time tracking down system crashes related to general protection faults, and thinking of ways to work around them.

PowerBuilder causes GPFs more frequently than other Microsoft Windows tools. There are two reasons for this problem. First, PowerBuilder has features which stretch the capabilities of development under Windows to the limit. Second, PowerBuilder suffers from inappropriate design and a lack of thorough testing by Powersoft.

On the other hand, some users say many of the problems could be related to Microsoft Windows itself. When Windows makes system calls to the underlying DOS OS, Windows applications can make conflicting demands on memory space, causing a GPF and system crash which forces the user to reboot. With the release of Microsoft's Windows 95, these problems have been solved and are no longer a concern.

Version 4.0 of PowerBuilder has various features to enable high-end AD in the C/S environment. These include multiplatform support, data pipeline support, and integration with a range of TP monitors.

Other PowerBuilder features, which will arrive in later releases will include tight integration with the Watcom compiler from Watcom International, of Waterloo, Ontario, Canada. This will allow for machine code compilation and the ability to generate C++ for other platforms such as UNIX or Microsoft Windows NT from within PowerBuilder.

Another new feature will be application partitioning which will allow developers to run portions of their PowerBuilder applications on Microsoft Windows or other platforms such as UNIX or Windows NT clients or servers. Future releases will include the ability to create and integrate remote services using PowerBuilder.

HarborView – from Harbor Software, Manchester, Massachusetts.

Harbor Software is a startup firm founded by Interbase Software Corp. founder Jim Starkey. HarborView provides developers and end-users with the ability to create applications using a visual programming language.

Applications are developed by building graphical representations of the procedures on the screen using icons, diagrams, and templates rather than parentheses, semicolons, and keywords. This makes it easier to use than other visual tools such as PowerBuilder from Powersoft, where coding in scripting language is necessary. HarborView does not require knowledge of traditional programming or 4GLs.

Users first define business rules using visual templates. Forms and reports are then created automatically from these rules. To change applications, users change the picture or graphical representation. HarborView will automatically rebuild the application.

HarborView is available on UNIX workstations from HP, Sun Microsystems, Inc., and IBM. It is also available on DEC's VMS boxes and UNIX PCs from The Santa Cruz Operation (SCO).

Build Momentum – from Sybase, Inc., Emeryville, California. Tel.: 510-596-3500.

This is a graphical, object-oriented C/S AD tool designed to support the Microsoft Windows, Apple Macintosh, and OSF/Motif environments. Features include:

- A multithreaded kernel that supports multitasking in the Build Momentum environment, even when the OS does not support multitasking;

- Automatic generation of the client and server portions of an application;

- Across-GUI platform support which takes a superset approach, optimizing all features and functions available in a given operating environment; and

- Automatic performance tuning to take advantage of any system configuration.

Build Momentum is part of the Momentum family of products from Sybase. The other two are Gain Momentum and Enterprise Momentum, both of which are object-oriented products.

Progress Version 7 – *from Progress Software Corp., Bedford, Massachusetts. Tel. 617-280-4000.*

Progress is an integrated, platform-independent environment for deploying and developing mission-critical applications which are scalable, portable, and reconfigurable across a wide range of computing environments, including C/S, host-based, and mixed environments.

It consists of the Progress AD Environment (ADE), the Progress DataServer Architecture, and the Progress RDBMS. The latest version, Version 7, was released in June 1993.

The Progress ADE is an integrated set of GUI-based tools for designing, implementing, testing, and deploying GUI and character-based applications for C/S and host-based systems.

The Progress DataServer Architecture is a set of services and interfaces that allow Progress applications to access a variety of DBMS and file systems, including the Progress RDBMS. The Progress RDBMS has been network-optimized for mission-critical TP applications. It delivers cross-platform scalability and a full set of administrative and tuning controls.

All Progress tools are based on the Progress 4GL which is a complete development language offering ANSI-standard SQL. It has an English-like syntax so developers can create applications in either GUI or character mode more quickly than in 3GL or scripting languages.

Progress Version 7 has an event-driven programming model which is fully integrated into the Progress 4GL. This lets Progress applications respond to user interface and database events. It also provides a common paradigm which enables developers to produce GUI applications with a look and feel native to that of applications already in use.

The programming model also allows developers to establish central business rules through the use of triggers. In addition, event-driven extensions reduce training time and provide a single language for users to build a complete application.

New features of Progress Version 7 include:

- *User Interface Builder* – this is the primary tool for building applications. In addition to allowing developers to paint their screens in either GUI or character mode, it lets them write or generate procedural Progress 4GL logic to handle computations or transactions and control application logic flow.

- *Application Debugger* – this facilitates the move to event-driven programming. It provides a complete set of facilities to help developers trace the flow of application execution, and locate and correct errors in application logic or data handling. The debugger has a graphical environment for testing all application components, and allows developers to view and change structures while running the applications.

- *Application HELP Development* – this feature lets developers use the word processor of their choice to develop help messages and fully integrate these messages into applications. HELP messages are portable across Microsoft Windows, OSF/Motif, and character modes.

- *Report Builder* – this is a graphical report writer for creating production-quality batch reports, designing a variety of report formats and user templates, addressing cross-database reporting needs, and producing portable report logic.

- *Translation Manager* – this automates much of the work required to localize an application for multiple spoken languages without requiring modification of the original source code or user interface.

Several features in previous versions of Progress have been enhanced in Version 7. These include:

- *Data Dictionary* – this serves as a central repository for all database definitions, business rules and application defaults, such as formats, labels, and the help feature. The Progress Version 7 ADE has been enhanced with two Dictionary interfaces: a fully graphical version for developers running Progress on graphical displays, and a character terminal version.

- *Procedure Editor* – this is a complete text editor which allows a programmer to graphically edit several 4GL programs simultaneously. It can also make global changes to data references and application logic quickly.

- *Progress Results* – this is an end-user data access and reporting tool which enables transparent access to heterogeneous data. It lets users with little or no programming experience satisfy their own ad hoc data retrieval and reporting requirements.

  Results employs a simple model for defining queries and reports. Users access menus to browse through a database, update the data and compile that information with other data, manipulate it mathematically and generate custom reports. Results can run in either character or graphical environments, and can integrate fully or partly into applications.

- *Application Open Interfaces* – these let Progress applications communicate with other applications and services through standard interfaces such as DDE, DLL, and Pipes. This lets mission-critical applications interact with personal productivity tools such as spreadsheets, graphics packages, and word processing packages, and also lets developers leverage third-party library functions for interfacing to outside devices or services.

The Progress DataServer's architecture consists of a set of data integration services which connect to database-specific DataServers. This lets Progress applications read from and write to a variety of databases and file systems, including the Progress RDBMS.

Progress DataServers can be used to access data stored locally on a host or remotely over a network. They provide database independence, data integration, and data migration. Version 7 will include DataServers for the following database and file managers: Oracle, Sybase, RMS, Rdb/VMS, C-ISAM, CT-ISAM, Object Store, DB2 (through DRDA), HP Allbase, and ODBC.

DataServer Open interfaces are central elements of the Progress DataServer architecture. They let Progress applications exchange information with other applications and system services to provide controlled access to information and allow configuration flexibility.

They are architected so that they can be extended in the future. Progress DataServers support a range of de facto and de jure industry standards.

The Progress RDBMS is a full-function, SQL-compliant relational database. It is optimized for mission-critical TP applications, and delivers cross-platform scalability and a full complement of administrative and tuning controls.

The Progress Version 7 RDBMS features enhanced capabilities for C/S environments. These include improved query optimization, reduced network traffic, database triggers, and word indexing. Other features are record-level locking, rollback and roll forward recovery, distributed database management with two-phase commit, online backup, ANSI standard SQL, and a multithreaded, multiserver architecture.

Progress Version 7 will be available on many platforms from leading vendors, including Data General, DEC, IBM, HP, ICL, Microsoft, NCR, Novell, SCO, Sequent, Silicon Graphics, Sun Microsystems, Unisys, and Univel.

Applications developed in Progress can be deployed across a variety of platforms without changes to the application code. The tools can be purchased separately from the database. The Progress RDBMS runs on more than 100 platforms and operating systems, ranging from PCs to multiprocessor minicomputers.

CA-DBFast 2.0 – from Computer Associates International, Inc., Islandia, New York. Tel. 516-342-5224.

Claiming to be the first and only dBASE-compatible database and language for Microsoft Windows, CA-DBFast 2.0 lets users move existing dBASE applications to the Microsoft Windows environment from XBase and develop new applications quickly.

It has a Visual Application Designer (VAD), a Workbench, and a compiler. The VAD lets users drag-and-drop or point-and-click to create radio buttons, push buttons, pull-down menus, check boxes, scrolling list boxes, and other Microsoft Windows objects. It generates the required source code. The VAD is data dictionary-based, and provides the framework for constructing a database.

The Workbench is a workspace providing the tools to create and modify data files, programs, and report forms. There are also tools for linking and running programs. A program editor lets developers create or edit program files, and there is a compiler which allows setting of preferences, compilation, and linking of program files into an executable file for running as a standalone Windows application.

CA-DBFast 2.0 includes a debugger which lets users watch the source code as it executes at runtime. It also includes CA-RET, a Microsoft Windows-based report writer which mixes text, graphics, and data on the same report in a full WYSIWYG environment. CA-dBFast 2.0 is compatible with CA-Clipper, dBase III Plus, dBASE IV, and FoxBASE.

Dialog System Professional – *from Micro Focus, Inc., Palo Alto, California. Tel. 415-856-4161.*

Dialog System Professional provides a user interface management system and application builder for developing GUIs for Microsoft Windows, OS/2, and character-based user interfaces for MS-DOS and OS/2.

The package supports development of new graphical applications using Micro Focus COBOL, and can be used to generate graphical front ends for existing CICS and IMS applications without the need for additional programming.

Techbridge Builder – *from Techbridge Technology Corp., North York, Ontario, Canada. Tel. 416-222-8998.*

Techbridge Builder is a GUI-based, object-oriented C/S AD environment for OS/2. It enables users to create workplace applications using drag-and-drop operations and enterprisewide database access.

It provides standard COBOL and SQL support, visual programming, business graphics support, and allows data to be converted to objects. Developers can test individual components as they are built, test groups of components, or test the entire application.

XFaceMaker 3.0 – from Non-standard Logics, Boston, Massachusetts. Tel. 617-482-6393.

XFaceMaker 3.0 is a GUI builder which lets users design both X/Window System intrinsics and C++ class libraries. It generates the skeleton of users' application code automatically with all initializations, memory allocation and function calls required by the interface. The package comes with a debugger which tests the behavior of the interface.

Features include dual-process architecture, fault tolerance, C++ class generation, a project management and application building module, and a database module.

GBB 3.0 – from Blackboard Technology Group, Inc., Amherst, Massachusetts. Tel. 413-256-8990.

GBB 3.0 is a framework for creating high-performance applications. It lets users create object-oriented GUI interfaces, which are source code-compatible, on all hardware platforms. Other features include an event mechanism and enhanced retrieval, tracing and metering.

Cross-Platform Graphic User Interface Development Tools

Wind/U – from Briston Technology, Ridgefield, Connecticut. Tel. 203-438-6969.

Wind/U supports Microsoft Windows and OSF/Motif GUIs. It maps Microsoft Windows calls to native X/Motif calls, letting Visual C++ applications created under Windows be ported to UNIX. Wind/U supports WinSoc API and ODBC through third-party add-ons.

CA-Realizer – *from Computer Associates International, Inc., Islandia, New York. Tel. 516-342-5224.*

CA-Realizer supports Microsoft Windows and OS/2. It emulates these GUIs and provides native GUI capabilities. This is accomplished by providing a map of the underlying GUI, and allowing direct access to each system API.

Its visual layout tool generates code based on design. The API allows third-party coding of a DLL to CA-Realizer.

SuperNova – *from Four Seasons Software, Edison, New Jersey. Tel. 908-248-6667.*

SuperNova supports Microsoft Windows, OSF/Motif, and Open Look. It runs on both the client and server for full application partitioning flexibility. It includes features such as the creation of classes, inheritance and polymorphism – standard object-oriented product features.

SuperNova offers native GUI widgets for each GUI environment, and offers AD using a visual application builder and/or its 4GL language. Third-party software supported includes any product with a C interface.

Omnis 7^3 – *from Blyth Software, Inc., Foster City, California. Tel. 415-571-0222.*

Omnis 7^3 is an enterprisewide C/S AD environment featuring true portability – developers can create an application once and then deploy it on a variety of platforms. It is aimed at large corporations with several divisions and teams of programmers.

Omnis 7^3 combines a visual programming interface with a development language. It has been designed to offer support across the entire AD lifecycle – prototyping, deployment, maintenance, change management, and automatic generation and distribution of upgrades. The product provides an enhanced data access architecture, extended middleware support, a developer's workbench, an SQL object browser, a SQL form builder, and a graphing tool. Its developer's workbench allows users to create and manage all objects required in front-end and back-end C/S applications.

The Omnis 7^3 Portable C/S Enterprise Kit includes both Microsoft Windows and Apple Macintosh cross-platform development environments, an unlimited application deployment license, and a nine-month warranty. Omnis 7^3 offers native look and feel for each platform.

Applications developed in Omnis 7^3 have three main components: program files, library files, and data files. The program file contains core functionality which can call upon extensions. Library files (data dictionaries) contain instructions on how the program data will be handled and presented, and can be used to store a variety of different formats. Finally, the data files consist of the user's data records and their indexes.

Omnis 7^3 has its own 4GL, written in C++. It does not have a compiler. The language provides an extension interface for use by advanced programmers; it also possesses what Blyth Software describes as an "object-like metasyntax," which is called the Omnis notation. The Omnis notation lets developers examine and amend objects called from within the Omnis 4GL. It also allows developers to write Omnis libraries which modify other Omnis libraries.

Omnis 7^3 can link up with 50 standard relational and non-relational databases through Omnis Connect. Omnis Connects are small modules written in C connecting Omnis 7^3 and the server API, or hooking Omnis 7^3 to third-party middleware which connects to the server.

Application library objects are reusable, and can be passed by core developers to other programmers. Libraries can be split into logical functional blocks containing all the file formats, windows, reports, menus and searches which would be used in a particular business area. All this encourages prototyping.

Omnis 7^3 offers change management and version control. It also supports application partitioning. It also supports multiuser networks. On the Apple Macintosh, the Apple Filing Protocol (AFP) is supported; on Microsoft Windows, OLE, and DDE are supported.

EISToolkit Version 2.11 – *from Microstrategy, Inc., Wilmington, Delaware. Tel. 302-427-8800.*

EISToolkit is a development environment for building applications for cross-platform, C/S EIS, and DSS. A programmer can use EISToolkit to create a graphical EIS which includes database management, graphs and controls, "what if" capabilities and modeling features for information analysis.

The product is based on Informix Corp.'s HyperScript 4GL and includes MicroStrategy's proprietary SQL Language Extensions. It is available for UNIX, Microsoft Windows, and Apple Macintosh.

JAM – from Jyacc, Inc., New York, New York. Tel. 212-267-7722.

JAM supports Microsoft Windows, OSF/Motif, Open Look, and SCO Open Desktop. It provides native GUI calls through Microsoft Corp.'s Visual Basic, and its visual interface layout tool uses the Visual Basic layout environment. JAM offers transparent distributed cache protocol to MS-DOS, UNIX and VMS servers using TCP/IP, IPX, NetBIOS, and serial networks. It works with any product that supports Visual Basic custom controls.

Smart Elements Version 2.0 – from Neuron Data, Inc., Palo Alto, California. Tel. 415-321-4488.

Smart Elements is a set of business rule development tools. The Smart Elements API has been enhanced in Version 2.0 to provide direct support for C++. This lets users link their C++ libraries and applications directly to applications written with Smart Elements, enabling integration of new and existing code.

Version 2.0 also features enhanced GUI design capabilities, including power widgets for business graphics, color icons and images, text-edit validation, Hypertext, and palettes. (A power widget is an object.) Other features include a data access element – which is a data connectivity option that enables developers to transparently access and manipulate data from multiple sources.

Smart Elements 2.0 emulates the native toolkit and supports native GUI calls. AD is conducted through the C/S Elements architecture. Extended support is offered through event-driven, object-oriented technology. Third-party software supported consists of middleware from Momentum, Inc., and testing tools from Mercury Interactive and Segue.

Smart Elements 2.0 runs under Microsoft Windows, Windows NT, Sun Solaris and SunOS, Digital OpenVMS, VAX VMS, OSF/1, Apple Macintosh, AIX on the IBM RS/6000, and HP/UX on HP computers.

Sapiens Ideo – *from Sapiens USA, Inc., Research Triangle Park, North Carolina. Tel. 919-405-1500.*

Ideo supports Microsoft Windows, Windows NT, OSF/Motif and Apple Macintosh. It uses native GUIs and it includes a GUI editor to build GUI windows while working in a graphical environment. Attributes of objects can be modified with SmartGL, a typeless SQL-based 4GL. The product provides an API with bidirectional calling facility to allow access to any third-party product with a 3GL API.

XVT Development Solution for C and C++ – *from XVT Software, Inc., Boulder, Colorado. Tel. 303-443-4223.*

XVT Development Solution for C and C++ supports Microsoft Windows, Windows NT, OS/2, Apple Macintosh, Open Look, and OSF/Motif. It offers a common GUI abstraction and API on top of native toolkits, and uses a visual layout tool. The product offers an object-oriented application framework for building applications.

Database connectivity and middleware are provided through XVT Partner technologies. Third-party software support includes application testing, builders, code analysis, database engines, and database connectivity.

Network Application Development Tools

AppWare – *from Novell, Inc., Provo, Utah. Tel. 801-429-7000.*

AppWare is a C/S AD suite which consists of the Visual AppBuilder graphical-based development front-end; AppWare Loadable Modules (ALMs) which are linked into a finished application; and the AppWare Foundation which Novell claims will screen developers from the underlying incompatibilities and complexities of client and network operating systems.

AppWare will have ALMs for:

- E-mail;

- SQL querying of several types of databases, including that from Gupta Corp.;

- Oracle Corp.'s imaging, calendering, reporting and messaging on the Apple Macintosh;

- Document management;

- Multimedia;

- Reporting and messaging on Microsoft Windows;

- Network management;

- Telephony; and

- A Tuxedo TP monitor (from Novell, Inc., Provo, Utah) for critical database applications.

Three Novell partners have announced AppWare support:

1. *Borland International*, of Scotts Valley, California, will support AppWare Foundation with its Object Windows Libraries. This will enable applications written with C++ development tools to be ported to other Foundation clients.

2. *WordPerfect Corp.*, of Orem, Utah, has endorsed AppWare as an enabling technology for its WordPerfect Office and other packages.

3. *Gupta Corp.*, of Menlo Park, California, has introduced a SQL-based ALM to be bundled with Visual AppBuilder, so that users can build small and prototype SQL-based query applications. The full version of Gupta's Visual AppBuilder is needed for larger applications.

When it was announced, AppWare was scheduled to support a variety of clients, including Microsoft Windows and Windows NT; as well as global directory services from Novell, Banyan Systems, Inc., and possibly other vendors.

However, there have been several recent developments in the AppWare field. Novell has purchased WordPerfect and has recently made major changes in its plans for AppWare. It has essentially dropped AppWare Foundation, which means it may not be able to offer multiplatform support. Although Novell will continue supporting AppWare Foundation for the next year or so, it has been privately advising users not to focus on it for business applications, according to media reports.

Instead, Novell will focus on Visual AppBuilder 1.0, and is seeking to leverage independent software vendors and its own WordPerfect Applications Group to promote the use of Visual AppBuilder. Already, PerfectOffice 3.0 bundles Visual AppBuilder with a library of PerfectOffice ALMs and the Visual AppBuilder tool.

Visual AppBuilder enables developers to create applications out of groups of ALMs. AppWare Foundation's ALMs will still be funded and supported, but the focus will be on Visual AppBuilder tools. Visual AppBuilder 1.0 includes about 80 ALMs, and comes with the AppWare Bus and the ALM Builder.

The AppWare Bus is a software engine which manages and coordinates the interaction of ALMs in a finished application; the ALM Builder lets developers create ALMs in C or C++ and use or reuse them as components in an AppBuilder application.

RPCware *– from NobleNet, Inc., Southborough, Massachusetts. Tel. 508-460-8222.*

RPCware generates NetWare Loadable Modules (NLMs) for building C/S applications on Novell networks.

Miscellaneous Application Development Tools

ClearCase MultiSite *– from Atria Software, Inc., Natick, Massachusetts. Tel. 508-650-1193.*

ClearCase is a software configuration management product for UNIX which supports parallel development and software reuse across geographically distributed development teams. It synchronizes versioned object bases on the basis of an update pattern selected by the software team at each location.

Features include a built-in store and forward system, standard UNIX file transfer facilities, and magnetic tape-based transfer.

Enterprise Developer – *from Symantec Corp., Cupertino, California. Tel. 408-253-9600.*

Enterprise Developer is a C/S AD tool for creating complex distributed database applications. It embeds the SQL database engine from XDB Systems, Inc. This is a database engine running under Microsoft Windows which provides 100% of IBM's DB2 SQL on the PC. The SQL engine includes an interactive SQL facility which allows users to interactively write SQL commands and edit data.

Enterprise Builder uses a centralized business model to reduce the time spent on all stages in the development cycle.

Ptech for Windows – *from Ptech, Inc., Westboro, Massachusetts. Tel. 508-366-9166.*

Ptech for Windows is a reengineering software package which provides active process models and generates complete ANSI-standard C++ applications. These models apply the rules directing a business process, so users can see how the total behavior of a process is affected when parts are changed.

Business processes modeled and generated by Ptech for Windows can be compiled on any computer with a standard C++ compiler.

Kipp Developer's Tool Kit 2.1 – *from Kofax Image Products, Inc., Irvine, California. Tel. 714-727-1733.*

Kipp Developer's Tool Kit 2.1 is a set of high-level C libraries designed for prototyping and developing production-level imaging applications. It lets developers add image scanning, compression, decompression, display, manipulation, file storing, image retrieval, and printing to existing or new applications. The product supports a number of high-speed scanners and printers.

Datarun – *from Computer Systems Advisors, Inc., Woodcliff Lake, New Jersey. Tel. 201-391-6500.*

Datarun is a methodology designed for groups building large, enterprisewide cross-functional applications. Features include rapid delivery of applications, a controlled, model-driven form of iterative development, and single-model development for close integration of data.

Huron – from Amdahl Corp., Santa Clara, California. Tel. 408-746-6000.

Huron is an applications system environment rather than just a tool. It gives both developers and users a simple, high-level interface for applications development, operations and maintenance. Applications written in Huron on one platform will execute in Huron on any other platform without recompiling. The approach used is evolutionary development, with developers and users jointly establishing the initial requirements, and creating prototype applications together, within days or weeks.

These prototypes are evolved directly into production systems, through interactive design reviews between the developers and users. As business requirements change, production-level Huron applications can be changed very easily using the same iterative process of having the developers and users work together.

Integrated into the Huron environment are a high-level rules language, an extended relational database, a dynamic data dictionary, a full set of programming tools and a variety of external database servers which provide transparent access to existing database management systems such as DB2, IDMS, IMS, VSAM, and Model 204. Huron also allows communication between Huron and non-Huron transactions. Most importantly, every implementation of Huron on a new platform extends the total Huron environment.

CA-Clipper – from Computer Associates International, Inc., Islandia, New York. Tel. 516-342-5224.

Version 5.2 of CA-Clipper is a robust language, an efficient linker, a flexible preprocessor and a high-performance compiler. It includes an editor, debugger and make utility for creating PC-based and LAN-based applications. It has replaceable database drivers for most database systems. This product can seamlessly integrate modules from languages such as C, Assembly, dBASE, and Pascal.

STP/IM – (Software Through Pictures / Information Modeling), from Interactive Development Environments, San Francisco, California. Tel. 415-543-0900.

STP/IM is the first robust UNIX information modeling tool set to provide comprehensive support for C/S development. It lets users build conceptual and logical models. STP/IM groups can generate SQL for relational database management systems and deploy the resulting applications on various platforms. STP/IM is available on SunSparc from Sun Microsystems, Inc.; HP 9000 Series 700 from HP; and RS/6000 workstations from IBM.

AD/Advantage – *from Cincom Systems, Inc., Cincinnati, Ohio. Tel. 513-662-2300.*

AD/Advantage, Cincom's application generation system, is a fully integrated, interactive environment which automates development activities in each phase of the AD lifecycle, thus improving productivity.

It generates C/S applications much faster than programmers can write them. AD/Advantage lets developers generate portable C/S applications for MVS, VSE, VM, most UNIX systems, Digital OpenVMS and OSF/1, DOS, OS/2 and other platforms. It supports strategic databases, including Cincom's Supra, IBM's DB2, DEC's Rdb, and Oracle Corp.'s Oracle.

The Philippine National Bank, headquartered in Manila, is moving from its mainframe-based computing environment to an open, C/S system with the help of AD/Advantage for SCO UNIX. Once the system is fully implemented, branches in Metro Manila will have online access to information from a consolidated database at headquarters which contains account profiles, referential and credit checks, and other management support information needed to monitor the bank's loans portfolio.

AD/Advantage for Windows – *from Cincom Systems, Inc., Cincinnati, Ohio. Tel. 513-662-2300.*

This is a comprehensive, PC-based AD and testing workbench for generating applications in a graphical environment. It also has all the features of AD/Advantage.

XpertRule – AD/Advantage – *from Cincom Systems, Inc., Cincinnati, Ohio. Tel. 513-662-2300.*

XpertRule is a Microsoft Windows-based knowledge specification and application generation system which allows users to quickly develop, prototype and refine applications requiring complex decision processes. It can be bought as part of the AD/Advantage system or as a standalone package.

XpertRule includes powerful knowledge structuring and rule induction facilities which can automatically generate Mantis or other structured code. (Mantis is a 4GL from Cincom.)

C++ Coder – *from Superbica, Astoria, New York. Tel. 718-728-5115.*

C++ Coder is a tool for Microsoft Windows which automatically generates C++ applications that run under Windows or OS/2. It can generate database and calculator programs, and C++ class libraries.

Users prepare simple tables describing each record in the application, and the product generates the code. (Up to 50,000 lines at a time can be generated.) C++ Coder comes with a test file generator, an automatic screen design feature, and an automatic documentation system which lets users create manuals up to 20 pages in length.

Energize Programming System 3.0 – *from Lucid, Inc., Menlo Park, California. Tel. 415-329-8400.*

Energize Programming System 3.0 is a UNIX programming tool that provides developers with the ability to work on a subset of a project, without having to manage the entire project in the workspace. This reduces resource requirements and protects the common code base.

The package is fully integrated with leading configuration management tools, and provides code understanding so that each developer on a team has the same view of the project code.

Energize Programming System 3.0 is available on Sun Microsystems, Inc.'s Solaris 2.x and SunOS 4.1.

Micro Focus CICS OS/2 Option Version 3.2 for Micro Focus COBOL Workbench – *from Micro Focus, Inc., Palo Alto, California. Tel. 415-856-4161.*

Micro Focus CICS OS/2 Option Version 3.2, for Micro Focus COBOL Workbench, is a development environment for mainframe and network-based CICS applications on OS/2.

It is a complete OLTP development system with distributed processing and multitasking capabilities. The product emulates mainframe CICS and provides a suite of development tools to create and maintain host-based or C/S CICS applications.

Features include: a development menu system, an integrated CICS preprocessor, single-step translation, compile and link processing, a macro generator, database support, and multisession debugging.

Micro Focus COBOL – *from Micro Focus, Inc., Palo Alto, California. Tel. 415-856-4161.*

Micro Focus COBOL is one of the most open systems in the industry. It lets programmers target applications to MS-DOS, Microsoft Windows, OS/2, and various implementations of UNIX. Micro Focus claims applications written in its COBOL package run as fast as anything written in C or C++, and faster than most 4GL-based applications.

Micro Focus COBOL has communications and data access capabilities which enable the development of cross-platform or C/S applications. Advanced tools such as Animator have been added to streamline source code debugging. The package has syntax extensions to handle GUIs, file and record locking and other functions.

Dialog System Professional, a RAD tool from Micro Focus, and OS/2 Revolve (the firm's systemwide analysis tool) have been added to Micro Focus COBOL. Object-orientation capability is available with Micro Focus' Object COBOL Option.

High C/C++ Compiler Version 3.2 for Windows NT – *from MetaWare, Inc., Santa Cruz, California. Tel. 408-429-6382.*

High C/C++ Compiler Version 3.2 for Windows NT produces Microsoft Windows NT-standard common object file format object modules and NT-standard CodeView-4 debugging information.

It has an Easy DLL feature which lets developers export or import functions in a given block of code. An EasyThread feature lets users convert existing routines and programs using Windows NT's multithreading capability.

High C/C++ Compiler includes the Win32 Enablement Package. This lets 32-bit applications created with High C/C++ run under Microsoft Windows 3.1.

***ENDEVOR/Workflow Manager for UNIX** – from Legent Corp., Herndon, Virginia. Tel. 703-708-3000.*

ENDEVOR/Workflow Manager for UNIX enables administrators and managers of software projects to standardize and control software development activities for the UNIX environment.

It brings the key functionality of ENDEVOR/MVS, Legent's software configuration management product for the mainframe, to the TeamTools software configuration management environment. (TeamTools are products for UNIX software development from TeamOne Systems, Inc., a company Legent acquired in February, 1994.)

ENDEVOR/Workflow Manager provides online package and approvals processing for the TeamTools UNIX-based software configuration management system. A package consists of a number of changes grouped together as a checkpoint in TeamTools. ENDEVOR/Workflow Manager allows only an approved administrator to work with the defined package, and ensures that the package is reviewed and approved before its changes are implemented.

Changes can be reversed or, once approved, made permanent. The product's capability to assign a designated approver during the review cycle gives managers the opportunity to standardize the approval process and prevent unauthorized code from going into production.

***Ellipse** – from Bachman Information Systems, Inc., Burlington, Massachusetts. Tel. 617-273-9003.*

This is a new version of the scalable C/S development tools offered to clients for development and production on Microsoft Windows or OS/2. Bachman acquired these tools from Cooperative Solutions, Inc. in 1993.

Chapter 12

Electronic Software Distribution

Overview

Some of the problems encountered when developing and distributing applications, such as version control and the actual distribution itself, can be resolved by turning to an electronic software distribution (ESD) package. As a process, ESD can be divided into three stages, according to market research firm The Gartner Group, Inc., of Stamford, Connecticut. These are electronic discovery, electronic delivery, installation, and configuration.

Electronic discovery is the feature which lets the ESD package determine what a corporation has in its computing environment, in terms of hardware and software. This is an essential part of both managing the computer system and ESD. Many ESD packages maintain a log of hardware and software in a table which they automatically update when changes are made.

Electronic delivery is just what it says. The ESD package delivers application software to servers and clients throughout a distributed network from the administrator's workstation. This does away with the need for traveling around to different departments or to remote sites to take the next step: installation and configuration.

There are two models for installation: the push model, and the pull model. In the push model, which is mainly used for applications developed in-house and

---

mission-critical applications, applications are sent out from a central site, usually the administrator's workstation, and installed on users' desktop PCs, whether or not they agree. In the pull model, more often used for shrink-wrapped applications bought off the shelf, the applications are sent to the local network server, and users pull down the ones they want.

The administrator can configure applications delivered, so that different applications are delivered to different PCs on a network, or different features are made available to different users, depending on their security clearance. All users may get a copy of a spreadsheet package, for example, but only those in the financial department will be able to tap into the corporate financial application; the others will have to use the spreadsheet locally.

Market Segments in Electronic Software Distribution

According to the Gartner Group, there are two distinct market segments in the ESD market: the enterprise software management segment; and the departmental, or so-called functional, segment.

Enterprise segment buyers want their ESD solution to cover most, if not all of the IT enterprise. This means the product must offer support for different platforms and protocols, such as SNA, TCP/IP, IPX, and robust configuration and installation management functionality. An enterprise solution must also be able to concurrently distribute software changes to more than 3,000 workstation and server targets.

Typically, central IT pays for the enterprise ESD solution, although initial funding may be from a departmental applications budget. Just because an ESD product sits on a mainframe does not mean it is an enterprise solution.

Departmental segment buyers look for ESD solutions which can effectively control software distribution within the boundaries of one or two applications contained within a large LAN or a corporate campus. Typical applications of departmental ESD solutions cover geographically contained environments with less than 2,000 distribution targets.

Pitfalls of Buying an Electronic Software Distribution Package

While an enterprise ESD package can also be used as a departmental solution, the reverse is not true. Take a careful look at the vendor literature, because there are many illegitimate claims to the enterprise ESD segment.

Some vendors are also marketing departmental solutions directly to senior business managers who lack the know-how to make a proper evaluation and come to the right decision.

According to the Gartner Group, the differences among the leading products in the departmental segment are not very clear, and there are too many vendors in this market. This will lead to heavy price competition and an eventual shakeout.

Planning for Electronic Software Distribution Purchases

Before deciding on any ESD solutions, IT organizations must define the scope of ESD coverage required. Implementing an ESD product takes six to nine months, inclusive of trial time, and payback begins six to nine months after the package is operational. To be a viable investment, therefore, the ESD solution picked must have an expected shelf life of about 24 months.

Electronic Software Distribution Vendors

Novadigm, Inc., Mahwah, New Jersey. Tel. 201-512-1000.

Novadigm offers EDM, a flexible, easily customized, enterprisewide distributed automation environment for deployment and configuration management and those shrink-wrapped applications developed in-house.

EDM builds object models of each desktop and server configuration. It tracks diverse configurations and handles a rapidly changing environment in which new technology and applications are being constantly introduced.

Novadigm says EDM lets users distribute, upgrade, and install software across geographically dispersed LANs and WANs servicing end-users running MS-DOS, Microsoft Windows, Apple Macintosh OS or OS/2 desktops. It sits on a central administrator's OS/2, Microsoft Windows or IBM 3270 Interactive System Production Facility (ISPF) workstation.

EDM uses the following networking protocols: Systems Network Architecture (SNA) from IBM; Novell NetWare; OS/2, or Microsoft Windows NT. Currently, EDM uses a mainframe MVS host as the distribution hub and object repository. Novadigm is working on a UNIX version of the package.

Legent Corp., Herndon, Virginia. Tel. 703-708-3000.

Legent offers two products: DistribuLink-MVS, for mainframes, and DistribuLink-UNIX. Both offer comprehensive management and control capabilities to perform automated and unattended software distribution to a variety of platforms, with complete reporting and audit trails.

DistribuLink-MVS is SAA-compliant and supports LU 6.2/APPC. The MVS server operates as a VTAM started task, and target nodes supported are OS/2, Microsoft Windows 3.1, PC-DOS, HP 9000, IBM RS/6000, Sun and Tandem. Support for the following target nodes will be added: NCR 3000, Sequent, MVS, AS/400, and others.

Network connections supported are SDLC, Coax, Ethernet, X.25, Token- Ring, asynch, autosynch, NetBIOS and IPX/SPX. The network connections are platform-dependent. Protocols supported are SNA to all platforms; TCP/IP will be supported in the future.

The server platform is MVS, and the administrator platform is OS/2. DistribuLink-UNIX runs on the following UNIX server platforms: IBM RS/6000 AIX; HP 9000 HP/UX from HP; Sun OS and Sun Solaris 2 from Sun Microsystems, Inc.; SCO UNIX, from The Santa Cruz Operation; DG AviiON, from Data General Corp.; and NCR 3000 AT&T S5R4 from AT&T/NCR.

Target systems supported are: PC-DOS, OS/2, Microsoft Windows 3.1, IBM RS/6000 AIX, HP 9000 HP/UX, SunOS, and Sun Solaris 2 from Sun Microsystems, Inc., SCO UNIX from The Santa Cruz Operation, NCR 3000 AT&T S5R4 from AT&T/NCR, and QNX. Windows NT will be added in the future.

Protocols supported include asynchronous and TCP/IP. Network connections supported include: asynchronous, direct connect, high-speed modem, satellite, TCP/IP, Ethernet, Token-Ring, and SLIP/PPP.

Frye Computer Systems, Inc., *Boston, Massachusetts. Tel. 617-451-5400.*

Frye offers The Frye Utilities for Networks – Software Update and Distribution System (SUDS) V1.5 and SUDS WAN Distribution (SUDSWAND) Module V1.0.

SUDS offers automated file updating, file replacement, and PC configuration management; updates MS-DOS and Microsoft Windows configurations; offers user distribution lists and a user menu of pull procedures; alarm notification options; a flexible PC selection capability; scheduling options; an undo feature; and user notification options. It also supports all major PC LANs. SUDS runs on an IBM PC, XT, AT, PS/2 or true compatible, under MS-DOS or PC-DOS 3.0 or higher, and requires 640 KB of RAM.

SUDSWAND automatically updates software throughout any size Novell network; creates routes for server-to-server distribution; allows local pre-distribution inspection; reports status of procedures; centralizes management of software distribution; and centralizes software and file distribution. It runs on an IBM PC, XT, AT, PS/2 or true compatible, under MS-DOS or PC-DOS 3.0 or higher, and requires 640 KB of RAM.

Microsoft Corp., *Redmond, Washington, has offices in various countries throughout the world.*

Microsoft offers SMS which is open, and leverages industry standards such as Desktop Management Interface (DMI) from the Desktop Management Task Force (DMTF). It was launched in late 1994, and runs on Daytona (Windows NT Advanced Server).

Five major tasks will be automated by SMS:

1. *Resource inventory.* SMS will collect detailed data on both hardware and software. It will support the definition of a hierarchy of management domains, and other ways of grouping and naming collections of workstations for use as targets of other functions.

2. *Scheduling and execution of remote maintenance activities on servers and desktops.* The most important activity is the distribution and installation of software and data packages; SMS will also have mechanisms for executing

remote programs and scripts, updating configuration files, and de-installing files.

3. *Establishing and updating desktop access to applications stored on servers.* SMS will set-up Windows Program Manager configurations to access the right application servers. It also supports server groups for load balancing.

4. *Remote control and troubleshooting of user PCs.*

5. *Centralizing C/S system monitoring through event-driven triggering of alert and diagnostic actions.*

Systems requirements for SMS are: Microsoft Windows NT Advanced Server version 3.5 or later; Microsoft SQL Server version 4.2 or later for Windows NT; a PC with an Intel 80486 CPU running at 50 MHz or faster; at least 32 MB of RAM; a hard disk with at least 100 MB of free space; a network-accessible CD-ROM drive; a network adapter card; and a mouse.

SMS is supported on the following networks: Microsoft Windows NT Advanced Server, Microsoft LAN Manager, and Novell NetWare. SMS supports the following WAN connection protocols: asynchronous, IPX/SPX, ISDN, SNA, TCP/IP, and X.25.

Clients supported are: MS-DOS 5.0 or later; Microsoft Windows 3.1 or later; Microsoft Windows NT version 3.1 or later; Microsoft Windows for Workgroups version 3.11 or later; Apple Macintosh System 7; and IBM OS/2 version 1.x or 2.x.

On Demand Software, *Naples, Florida. Tel. 813-261-6678. E-mail 74347.137@compuserve.com.*

On Demand distributes WinINSTALL version 4.0 from Aleph Takoma Systems, Inc. A true Microsoft Windows application, WinINSTALL captures the setup parameters of a Windows application installation, and handles every aspect of Windows application setup, including what files to copy, .INI file changes, icon installation, program groups, and OLE registration.

Installations can be tailored to fit user corporations' requirements, letting corporations come up with a customized list of standard applications that can be installed, uninstalled or upgraded over the network.

WinINSTALL offers three methods of installing, uninstalling, and upgrading applications.

1. *User-driven.* End-users can run the interactive WinINSTALL program, which is a Windows application providing a scrollable list of applications available for installation, an install button, a remove button, and an exit button. By clicking the mouse, the user launches the automatic installation of an application. The application will be installed exactly as configured by the LAN administrator.

2. *Centrally driven.* The WinINSTALL/AutoProgram is placed in an end-user's Win.INI Run = line or Windows 3.1 Startup Group. This initiates a configuration check each time the user starts Windows – WinINSTALL compares the list of available applications to those installed on the user's PC. Those which have not been installed will be installed automatically; if all available applications are already installed, WinINSTALL terminates itself at once, without appearing on the user's display.

3. *Through E-mail.* The WinINSTALL Administrative Program can create installation modules for sending electronic mail attachments through any Windows-based E-mail system. When creating the module, the administrator specifies whether the software is being installed, uninstalled, or upgraded. The WinINSTALL/AutoProgram is automatically launched when a user double-clicks on the attachment in the received mail message, triggering an immediate software install, uninstall or upgrade.

Symantec Corp., *Cupertino, California. Tel. 408-253-9600.*

Symantec Corp. offers Norton Administrator for Networks 1.0 (NAN). NAN is network-independent, and claims to be the only product which lets users add and administer Norton AntiVirus for NetWare from the console.

It also allows users to incorporate Norton pcANYWHERE (a remote communications program) into the console, to reduce the time spent on end-user application support and troubleshooting.

NAN takes hardware and software inventory, meters application usage and licensing, performs software distribution, and offers reporting and charting. Distribution options include scheduling, end-user messages, automatic reboot of workstations when distribution is completed, automated file update, replace or remove, group/distribution list support, undo, backup files, priority jobs, and record/playback. A script language is included to fully automate software installations.

System requirements for a Windows Console are a minimum of 5 MB of disk space and 2 MB of RAM, Windows 3.1-compatible in standard or enhanced mode. A server requires at least 8.5 MB of disk space, Novell NetWare 2.1.5, 2.2, 3.1.1 or 4.0 (except 4.0 Directory Services), Microsoft LAN Manager 2.1 and above or Banyan Vines 4.5 and above, including StreetTalk.

DOS workstations will need at least 640 KB of RAM, and must run MS-DOS 3.31 and above, including DOS 6.0. Windows workstations need at least 2 MB of RAM and have to be Windows 3.1-compatible in standard or enhanced mode.

Symantec and HP will integrate NAN into the HP OpenView for Windows environment by the end of 1994. This will bring end-user resource management tools to the HP OpenView for Windows console.

Chapter 13

Conclusion

Before a corporation begins AD, it must make sure that MIS develops a strategic plan which is aligned with the corporate business plan. Then, MIS has to make sure that it selects an AD environment rather than getting individual tools. This environment must meet certain criteria – scalability, flexibility, software lifecycle support, and programmer-productivity technologies.

Once this has been done, the development team has to be selected. This requires careful work, and it is best to select people with a good mix of skills. At least one member of the team should have classical programming skills, so that he or she can give the group direction and ensure the project adheres to programming disciplines.

Thought must also be given to standardization. The concept of a Corporate API should be explored, and once a corporate API is worked out, it should then be enforced.

The duties of line MIS and central MIS must be addressed. Programmers who are sent to business departments constitute line MIS; those who remain in the glass house constitute central MIS. While central MIS sets the overall strategy, line MIS deals with the tactical issues. Eventually, these groups work hand-in-hand, and an arbitration panel, consisting of top representatives from all corporate departments is set-up to arbitrate any disputes which may arise between them.

Before actual programming work begins, the application must be designed. This is the time to develop the testing plan. It is important to begin testing as early as possible in the development cycle, because it is always less expensive and easier to correct mistakes early in the process. Testing should support the entire lifecycle.

Of the various methodologies for development – CASE, 4GL, object, GUI/graphical – there is no one methodology which is better than the others, except subjectively. In other words, if a particular methodology best suits the needs of the corporation, then that is the methodology which must be selected – provided it allows room for growth in the future.

Finally, MIS must consider the question of automation. Automating tests frees programmers to concentrate on more productive activities and enhances the accuracy of testing. Automating software distribution and version control, through the use of electronic software distribution tools, also allows programmers to be more productive and makes version control and software distribution easier.

In short, AD is a task which needs careful planning and consideration at every step to succeed. Thorough planning and careful checking will go a long way toward minimizing costs when developing applications.

Glossary

ALM *AppWare Loadable Module.* A plug-in component from Novell, Inc.'s AppWare C/S application development suite.

API *Application Programming Interface.* This is a set of parameters which enable standardization of application development.

Abstract class. A class which can be used only as a base class of some other class. No objects of an abstract class can be created except as instances of a subclass. An abstract class is typically used to define a common interface for a number of subclasses.

Abstract data type. A data type which is specific to a particular kind of application, and representative of a real-world entity.

Abstraction. The logical form which analogous things have in common. Also, the process of identifying the characteristics which distinguish a collection of similar objects; the result of the process of abstraction is a type.

Application. The definition, design, construction and running of a business process through software development.

Architecture. A structured, modeled collection of services and their interfaces to the external environment. Provides guidelines or rules for the design and construction of a system. The software architecture of a system is defined by the classes and the interrelation of the classes; the hardware architecture is determined by the arrangement of the hardware and software components.

ASCII *American Standard Code for Information Exchange.* Used for the representation of alphanumeric information within a computer. ASCII is an 8-bit code in which seven bits indicate the character represented, and the eighth (high-order) bit is used for parity. Most commonly used on microcomputers and large non-IBM computers.

Asynchronous. A process which occurs without having to wait for another process to complete.

Attribute. A named property or characteristic of an entity. Usually represented as a field in a row of a database table.

Business rules. Constraints or actions which refer to the actual commercial world, not the computer environment.

CUA *Common User Access.* An IBM standard.

CASE *Computer Aided Software Engineering.* Systems development methodologies to assist in modeling and creating applications and systems.

CICS *Customer Information Control System.*

Class. The metadata (definition) for a class of objects. Attributes and methods will typically be defined within an object class.

Class libraries. Collections of pre-built, pre-tested objects which can be assembled into applications.

Client. A process that uses the services of independent processes. Communicates with a server, or multiple servers, by sending requests to the server.

COM *Common Object Model.* The object model behind Microsoft Corp.'s Object Linking and Embedding (OLE).

Compiler. A piece, or pieces of software, which accepts a programming language (such as Fortran or COBOL) and uses it to generate machine code.

DBMS *Database Management System.*

DCE *Distributed Computing Environment.* From OSF, the Open Software Foundation.

DDE *Dynamic Data Exchange.*

DLL *Dynamic Link Library.*

Data dictionary. Also called a library, it is a list of all data types used in a computer system. It is used in connection with a database management system which correlates names with databases. If, for example, a programmer furnishes the name "Phone.Number," the DBMS will look it up in the data dictionary to obtain the actual filename of the database containing telephone numbers. Increasingly, data dictionaries are being replaced by repositories. The data dictionary contains raw data, while the repository cross-references this information, analyzes it and adds meaning to it.

Decision support. An application optimized to allow end-users to receive information within databases in an accessible form to enable decision making.

Distributed processing. The running of applications across multiple platforms in a decentralized, as opposed to centralized, environment. Client/server is one type of distributed processing.

EBCDIC *Extended Binary Coded Decimal Interchange Code.* An 8-bit code for representing alphanumeric information within a computer. Used in large systems.

ESD *Electronic Software Distribution.*

Embedding. An object that contains a non-object value. The purpose of embedding is to enable software entities, or applications, to operate in an object-oriented environment.

Encapsulation.   Combining data, and the functions that affect data, into a single object.

Encyclopedia.   Another name for repository. Refers to a storehouse for all an organization's business policies and strategies, and information on all its systems. Metadata, or information about information in a corporation's computer system, is stored in the encyclopedia.

Enterprise computing.   Refers to all the resources (hardware, software, and personnel) which comprise a business and its processing requirements.

Entity.   A person, place or concept about which an organization chooses to store data. Entity models of an organization are usually created during the system design process and used to design databases, with the entities having corresponding tables in the databases.

Event.   A measurable occurrence within a computer system during processing which often involves one program calling upon another for service. When a computer adds two numbers together, that is not an event because it is handled entirely by the CPU; however, a mouse click or pulling down a menu or reading data from a disk is an event because the executing program calls on another program to execute its task.

Event-driven programming.   Where an application is developed so that it responds to events rather than to the timing or sequence of occurrences in the execution of a program.

GUI   *Graphical User Interface.*

ISV   *Independent Software Vendor.* An ISV is a third-party software developer and vendor which creates applications that run on various hardware platforms or supplement software created and sold by large software vendors.

Inheritance.   A relationship between classes which enables the reuse of code and the definition of a generalized interface to one or more sub-classes; the ability of one object in one class to pass its attributes to a second object in a lower class. In an inheritance relationship, the general class is the superclass and the specific class the subclass.

Interface. The portion of an object that is accessible to external software agents. In object-oriented programming, an interface is the set of requests which applies to a class.

Interoperability. The ability of a software product to interface with many other products.

LAN *Local Area Network.*

Legacy applications. Applications that are developed for, and run on, minicomputers or mainframe computers.

Library. Also called a data dictionary, it is a list of all data types used in a computer system.

Messaging. The means by which objects communicate with one another.

Metadata. Information about information contained in a corporation's computer system. Stored in the repository.

Method. An implementation of a behavior or a type; the specific implementation of an operation for a class; code which can be executed in response to a request. A method can extend or override the behavior defined in the operation. In many systems, the selection of a specific method to respond to a request can be done at compilation or execution.

Methodology. An attempt to encapsulate the software production process, or some part of it, within a predefined method.

Middleware. Connectivity software used to provide data access capability in a client/server environment.

Mission-critical application. Any application which is essential to the business of a corporation, such as a financial application or a manufacturing application.

Model. A representation of a problem or subject area which uses abstraction to express concepts. A model is often a collection of schemata and other documentation.

Model-driven development.   Used in client/server application development. Because client/server applications are far more complex than traditional applications, business models must be used to model this complexity so developers and users can focus on automation of the business process, rather than on the underlying technology or application style.

Module.   A collection of objects, methods and classes which collaborate to provide a subset of the functionality of an application. Modules can retain their own state and share information with the rest of the application.

Multithreaded.   A process which can support a number of users but has only one copy of the object code in memory.

Non-procedural language.   A language where the order of statements is not important, and where there is an emphasis on what is to be done rather than how it is to be done. Most event-driven languages are less procedural.

ODBC   *Open Database Connectivity.* An application programming interface for creating links between different relational and other databases which is backed by Microsoft Corp.

OLE   *Object Linking and Embedding.* This is Microsoft Corp.'s implementation of object-oriented technology.

OLTP   *Online Transaction Processing.*

OOP   *Object-oriented Programming.*

ORB   *Object Request Broker.* A software mechanism by which objects make and receive requests and responses.

Objects.   Software packages containing a collection of related procedures and data.

Object-based.   Any method, language or system which supports object identity, classification and encapsulation. An object-based system does not support specialization.

Object-oriented. Any method, language or system which supports object identity, classification, encapsulation and specialization. C++, Smalltalk, Objective-C and Eiffel are examples of object-oriented implementation languages.

Object-oriented programming. A procedure to combine objects with systems procedures to develop an application. Key elements are inheritance, data abstraction and encapsulation.

Object type. An abstraction (predicate) which can apply to a collection of objects. It is the logical form of a collection of analogous objects. An object type is an idea or notion which can be determined to apply, or not to apply, to an object. It classifies objects according to meaningful properties and behavior.

Open systems. Systems based on standards which are widely accepted, either by standards organizations or by de facto industry standards, and which have applications that can run on different platforms.

Polymorphism. A request-handling mechanism which selects a method based on the type of the target object. This allows the specification of one request which can result in the invocation of different methods, depending on the type of the target object. Most object-oriented languages support the selection of the appropriate method based on the class of the object. This is known as classical polymorphism. A few languages or systems, however, support generalized polymorphism. This is method selection based on other characteristics of the object than the class, such as values and user-defined defaults.

Portability. The ability to move an application environment from one hardware platform to another.

Precompiler. A piece of software which converts SQL statements into a native data manipulation language that a computer can recognize.

Preprocessing. The act of submitting a program containing SQL statements to a pre-compiler.

Procedural language. A language where the order of statements is important, and where the emphasis is on *how* things are done, rather than *what* is done.

Prototyping. Developing a system based on small components of the entire application. A prototype is presented to end-users as a working model of a much larger application.

RDBMS *Relational Database Management System.* An RDBMS is designed to store and retrieve data as a set of tables. The appearance of two or more data elements in a single row of a table is a "relationship" of those data elements.

RPC *Remote Procedure Call.* Synchronizes the processing of a client and a server.

Report writers. Tools which enable end-users to access data and develop reports which will address their jobs, without requiring the help of MIS.

Repository. Also called an encyclopedia. Refers to a storehouse for all an organization's business policies and strategies, and information on all its systems. A repository acts as an index describing all the metadata, or information about information, contained in a computer system.

Request. An event which is the invocation of an operation. The request includes the operation name and zero or more actual parameters. A client issues a request to cause a service to be performed. Requests are also associated with the results that can be returned to the client. A message can be used to implement (carry) the request and any results.

SAA *Systems Application Architecture.* An IBM worldview.

SQL *Structured Query Language.* A high-level DBMS query language defined in ANSI Standard X3.135. It is a standard non-procedural data definition and manipulation language for RDBMSs.

Scalability. The ability of an application to run on larger platforms or perform tasks on a larger scale than the one for which it was designed.

Server. A process which provides data, peripherals or services to other independent processes.

Stored Procedure. Application logic developed with a procedural language and stored in the database. The procedures can be shared among clients and are not database-function specific. They can express general procedural logic. However, stored procedure languages are specific to each database vendor.

Synchronous. A process which must wait for another process to complete before it can complete.

Table. A representation of data where the data is arranged as a two-dimensional array of columns and rows.

Transaction. A unit of work, usually a single unit of interaction with a database.

TCP/IP *Transmission Control Protocol/Internet Protocol.* One of the most commonly used protocols in mainframe environments, and the one used by the Internet.

WAN *Wide Area Network.*

3GL *Third Generation Language.*

4GL *Fourth Generation Language.*

Appendix B

References

Anthes, G. H. "Stress Test for Systems." *Computerworld*, May 17, 1993. Pp. 71, 75.

Argila, Carl A. "The OOP Survival Guide." *Computerworld*, Aug. 22, 1994. Pp. 89, 92-3.

Ballou, Melinda-Carol. "Customers Fret Despite KnowledgeWare Merger." *Computerworld*, Aug. 15, 1994. P. 71.

Ballou, Melinda-Carol. "HarborView Promises Visual Development." *Computerworld*, Oct. 18, 1993. P. 95.

Ballou, Melinda-Carol. "LBMS Smooths Link to PowerBuilder." *Computerworld*, Oct. 18, 1993. P. 101.

Ballou, Melinda-Carol and Johnston, Stuart. "Novell Changes Gears on AppWare Plans." *Computerworld*, Sept. 5, 1994. P. 7.

Ballou, Melinda-Carol. "Object Standards Accelerate." *Computerworld*, Sept. 5, 1994. Pp. 1, 14.

Ballou, Melinda-Carroll. "Powersoft Catches User Flak." *Computerworld*, Aug. 22, 1994. Pp. 1, 117.

Ballou, Melinda-Carol. "Vendor Targets Client/Server." *Computerworld*, Oct. 18, 1993. P. 96.

"Building the Case for the Quality of Your GUI, Client/Server Applications" – white paper. Softbridge, Inc., Cambridge, MA.

Caldwell, Bruce. "The Five Percent Solution." *Information Week*, Aug. 8, 1994. P. 59.

Cook, T.W. "Retraining Business Organizations for the Object-Oriented Era." *First Class*, The Object Management Group Newsletter, March/April 1994. Pp. 11, 17.

Cummins, Fred A. and Ibrahim, Mamdouh H. "Wrapping Legacy Applications." *First Class*, The Object Management Group Newsletter, March/April 1994. Pp. 10, 20.

Darling, Charlie. "PowerBuilder, PowerMaker Ease Transition to Objects." Reviews, *Infoworld*, Nov. 15, 1993. Pp. 153-7.

Dix, Heidi S. and Woodring, Stuart D. "Software Standards or Chaos?." *The Software Strategy Report*, Sept. 1993. Forrester Research, Inc., One Brattle Square, Cambridge, MA 02138. Tel.: 617-497-7090.

Eckerson, Wayne. "Bluestone Uses Objects to Link Clients and Data Servers." Network World, Oct. 11, 1993. P. 34.

Eckerson, Wayne. "Intersolv Enters GUI Client/Server Tool Mart." *Network World*, Nov. 8, 1993. P. 9.

Eckerson, Wayne. "NobleNet RPC Compiler Speeds Apps Development." *Network World*, Nov. 8, 1993. P. 9.

Fryer, Bronwyn. "Object Lesson: OLE and OpenDoc are Battling for Developers' Mind Share." *Computerworld*, Aug. 15, 1994. P. 107.

"Glossary of Terms." Object Technology, a white paper from the Object Management Group.

Grantham, Tim. "Bank Vaults Into World of Objects." *Computerworld*, Oct. 11, 1993. Pp. 69, 76.

Herman, James. "Microsoft Hermes: The Recipe for Enterprise Management for Client/Server Computing from Redmond." *Distributed Computing Monitor*, Vol. 9, No. 3, March, 1994. Editor-in-chief: John R. Rymer. Herman can be contacted at 415-296-7744.

Herman, James, vice president, Northeast Consulting Resources, Inc. (Boston, MA) "Novadigm's Enterprise Desktop Manager." Herman can be contacted at 415-296-7744.

Implementing CASE Technology. Computer Technology Research Corp., Charleston, SC, 1990.

Kay, Emily. "Code That's Ready to Go." *Information Week*, Aug. 22, 1994. Pp. 54, 56, 60, 61.

Kelly, David A. "10 Tips for Terrific GUIs." *Computerworld*, Aug. 1, 1994. P. 80.

Kernochan, Wayne. "The Right Criteria for Choosing a Client/Server Application Development Environment" – an Executive White Paper, May 1994. The Aberdeen Group, Inc., One Boston Place, Boston, MA 02108. Tel.: 617-723-7890; fax: 617-723-7897.

Korzeniowski, Paul. "Building Blocks for a New Age." *Information Week*, July 25, 1994. Pp. 62-70.

Korzeniowski, Paul. "Vendors are Teaming to Make Better Tools: Applications Development and CASE Tools Offer More Efficiency When Linked." *Information Week*, July 25, 1994. P. 72.

Larocque, Judy. "Object World Boston '94 Survey Results." *First Class*, The Object Management Group Newsletter, March/April 1994. Pp. 5, 17.

Mezick, Daniel. "Innovative Visual Basic Tools Sell as Shareware." *Infoworld*, Nov. 15, 1993. P. 177.

Nash, Kim S. "Andersen Gains Object Advantage." *Computerworld*, May 17, 1993. P. 71.

Oracle Cooperative Development Environment Technology Audit. The Butler Group. Development Tools Series No. 35. June, 1993.

Panepinto, Joe. "Client/Server Breakdown." *Computerworld*, Oct. 4, 1993. Pp. 107, 110, 111.

Potter, Carl and Cory, Dr. Therese. *Client/Server Development Tools: An Evaluation and Comparison.* Robin Bloor and Tom Jowitt, eds. Butler Bloor Ltd. Milton Keynes, U.K., 1993.

Radding, Alan. "Repository Van Winkle." *Client/Server Computing*, Aug. 1994. Pp. 60-61, 63-64.

Runge, Bob. "Building Business With Sybase Momentum." *Sybase Magazine*, Winter, 1994. Pp. 20-25.

"The Softbridge Automated Test Facility Product Overview." A white paper from Softbridge, Inc., 125 Cambridge Park Drive, Cambridge, MA 02140. Tel.: 617-576-2257; fax: 617-864-7747.

"Sybase Momentum Tools Debut." *Sybase Magazine*, Winter, 1994. P. 15.

Vizard, Michael. "Q&E Tool Sings Visual Basic Tune." *Computerworld*, Oct. 18, 1993. P. 104.

Weitz, Lori. "More and More Companies Have a Cross-Platform to Bear." *Client/Server Computing*, Aug. 1994. Pp. 51-54, 56-57.

Woodring, Stuart D. and DePalma, Donald A. "Building a Corporate API." *The Software Strategy Report*, Mar. 1993. Forrester Research, Inc., One Brattle Square, Cambridge, MA 02138. Tel.: 617-497-7090.

Interview with Naresh Bala, Product Marketing Manager for Testing Product Line, CenterLine Software, Inc. CenterLine Software is at 10 Fawcett St., Cambridge, Massachusetts 02138-1110. U.S. Inquiries: Tel. 617-498-3000; International Inquiries: Tel. 617-498-3277.

Interview with Bruce Hall, Senior Product Manager, Software Administration Division, Legent Corp., Herndon, Virginia.

Interview with Linda Hayes, CEO and President, AutoTester, Inc., Dallas, Texas.

Interview with Herb Isenberg, Technical Lead, Testing Services, Charles Schwab & Co., Inc., San Francisco, California.

Interview with Peter Klante, Vice President, Client/Server Tools Business Unit, Cognos, Inc. P.O. Box 9707, 3755 Riverside Drive, Ottawa, Ontario, Canada K1G 3Z4. Tel.: 617-229-6600 (sales, service and marketing).

Computer Technology Research Corp.

6 North Atlantic Wharf, Charleston, South Carolina 29401 U.S.A. • Tel: 803/853-6460; Fax: 803/853-7210

REPORT EVALUATION

Dear valued customer:

It is our continued desire and top priority to provide you with the most current and accurate computer technology information in our reports. Please assist us by taking a few minutes to answer the enclosed questionnaire. Your participation will help us to continue to provide professional service and quality reports to you. Please return the completed questionnaire by fax or mail. Feel free to attach additional sheets if you would like to add more comments. Your time and input are greatly appreciated.

Sincerely,

Edward R. Wagner

Edward R. Wagner
President

Report Title:

Customer Name:

Address/Phone:

Rating System: 1=poor, 2=fair, 3=good, 4=above average, 5=outstanding	1	2	3	4	5
1. How would you rate your overall satisfaction with this report?	☐	☐	☐	☐	☐
2. How would you rate the informational content?	☐	☐	☐	☐	☐
3. How would you rate the technical content?	☐	☐	☐	☐	☐
4. Overall, how up-to-date is the report?	☐	☐	☐	☐	☐
How would you rate the quality of data provided regarding: a) product releases?	☐	☐	☐	☐	☐
b) price/performance data?	☐	☐	☐	☐	☐
c) product evaluations?	☐	☐	☐	☐	☐
d) management issues?	☐	☐	☐	☐	☐
5. How would you rate the quantity of illustrations?	☐	☐	☐	☐	☐
6. How would you rate the quality of illustrations?	☐	☐	☐	☐	☐
7. To what degree did this report provide the information which you were desiring to obtain on the subject matter?	☐	☐	☐	☐	☐

Continued on next page

Rating System: 1=poor, 2=fair, 3=good, 4=above average, 5=outstanding	1	2	3	4	5
8. How would you rate the readability of the report in terms of general appearance (type style, layout, etc.)?	☐	☐	☐	☐	☐
9. How would you rate the report's international coverage?	☐	☐	☐	☐	☐
10. To what extent will the material in this report figure into your decision-making?	☐	☐	☐	☐	☐
11. To what extent did you save time or money by reading this report? (Please explain briefly if possible)	☐	☐	☐	☐	☐
12. Is this the first CTR report you have purchased?		Yes ☐		No ☐	
13. Would you purchase other CTR reports?		Yes ☐		No ☐	
14. Would you recommend that other information technology professionals purchase this report?		Yes ☐		No ☐	
15. Do you believe the information provided warrants the report's cost?		Yes ☐		No ☐	
16. Were you satisfied with the service you received from our staff in fulfillment of your order?		Yes ☐		No ☐	
17. Did your shipment arrive in good condition?		Yes ☐		No ☐	
18. Were you satisfied with the delivery time of your shipment?		Yes ☐		No ☐	
19. What additional information or topics would you have desired to see in this report that were not adequately covered?					
20. What topics would you like to see us cover in future reports?					
21. If you know of another individual whom you believe would be interested in receiving information concerning our report series, please list his/her full mailing address below:					

Mail or fax your completed questionnaire to: **Computer Technology Research Corp.**
6 North Atlantic Wharf
Charleston, SC 29401-2150 U.S.A.
Fax: (803) 853-7210

Thank you for your time and input!